Bangkok and Surrounds

0   20 km
    20 miles

N

Ayutthaya **15**

Song Phi Nong

Bridge on the River Kwai
13 Kanchanaburi

Pathum Thani

Thanyaburi

Don Tum

Bang Bua Thong

Don Muang

Lam Luk Ka

Ban Pong

Nakhon Pathom

Nonthaburi

Bang Phae

Taling Chan

Rose Garden

Thonburi

Bangkok

Photharam

Krathum Baen

12

Chachoengsao

Ratchaburi

Samut Sakhon

Phra Pradaeng

Samut Prakan

14

Phanat Nikhom

Floating Market

Samut Songkhram

Chonburi

Nakhon Khiri
Phetchaburi **1**

Gulf of Thailand

Si Racha

Bang Lamung

Ko Phai

Pattaya **18**

Nong Nooch Village

Ko Khram

Sattahip

Rayong

Hua Hin **17**

Th. Phaya Thai

Jim Thompson House Museum

Srapathum Palace

Th. New Phetchaburi

Th. Rama I

Siam Centre

Siam Paragon

Central World

Mah Boon Krong (MBK)

Soi Chulalongkorn 12

Th. Rama I

Erawan Shrine

Th. Ploenchit

PATHUMWAN

Th. Phaya Thai

Royal Bangkok Sports Club (R.B.S.C.)

Soi Lang Suan

Th. Withayu

Chulalongkorn University

Rama IV

Queen Saovabha Memorial Institute (Snake Farm)

SUAN LUMPHINI

Thanon Si Praya

Thanon Withayu

Chalerm Mahanakhon Expressway

7

Lumphini Boxing Stadium

Thanon Surawong

Th. Rama IV

PATPONG

Th. Silom

Thanon Sathorn Nua

Thanon Sathorn Tai

D1365431

INSIGHT GUIDES

BANGKOK
StepbyStep

APA PUBLICATIONS **L**

Part of the Langenscheidt Publishing Group

CONTENTS

Blue Elephant

ABOUT THIS BOOK

This *Step by Step Guide* has been produced by the editors of Insight Guides, whose books have set the standard for visual travel guides since 1970. With top-quality photography and authoritative recommendations, this guidebook brings you the very best of Bangkok in a series of 18 tailor-made tours.

WALKS AND TOURS

The tours in the book provide something to suit all budgets, tastes and trip lengths. Whether you are a gourmet or hungrier for cultural attractions, passionate about shopping, or prefer to chill out at the beach, you will find an option to suit. As well as covering Bangkok's many classic attractions, the routes track lesser-known sights and up-and-coming areas; there are also excursions for those who want to extend their visit outside the city.

We recommend that you read the whole of a tour before setting out. This should help you to familiarise yourself with the route and enable you to plan where to stop for refreshments – options for this are shown in the

'Food and Drink' boxes, recognisable by the knife-and-fork sign, on most pages.

For our pick of the walks by theme, consult Recommended Tours For… *(see pp.6–7).*

OVERVIEW

The tours are set in context by this introductory section, giving an overview of the city to set the scene, plus background information on food and drink, shopping and nightlife. A succinct history timeline at the end of this chapter highlights the key events that have shaped Bangkok over the centuries.

DIRECTORY

Also supporting the tours is a Directory chapter, comprising a user-friendly, clearly organised A–Z of practical information, our pick of where to stay, and select restaurant listings that complement the more low-key cafés and restaurants featured within the tours themselves and offer a wider choice for evening dining. There is also a brief selection of Bangkok nightspots.

Above: Abhisek Dusit Throne Hall; seated Buddha images in Wat Suthat; longtail boat; Calypso Cabaret at the Asia Hotel; nighttime Bangkok by tuk tuk.

The Author

Howard Richardson lives beside Bangkok's Chao Phraya River, and has spent the last 12 years exploring the city as a magazine editor and freelance writer, tackling subjects ranging from Buddhism to Elvis Presley impersonators. He wrote a monthly column for six years on Bangkok events and trends in *Sawasdee*, the Thai Airways in-flight magazine, and until 2002 was the editor of Thailand's then biggest-selling English-language magazine, *Bangkok Metro*. An award-winning feature writer, he has also contributed pieces on food for the BBC's *Olive* magazine and on nightlife for *GQ*. When he is not writing, he relaxes at the drum kit in a blues, funk and jazz band.

Margin Tips

Shopping tips, historical facts, handy hints and information on activities help visitors to Bangkok make the most of their time in the city.

Feature Boxes

Notable topics are highlighted in these special boxes.

Key Facts Box

This box gives details of the distance covered on the tour, plus an estimate of how long it should take. It also states where the tour starts and finishes, and gives key travel information such as which days are best to do the tour or handy transport tips.

Route Map

Detailed cartography shows the tour clearly plotted with numbered dots. For more detailed mapping, see the pull-out map slotted inside the back cover.

Food and Drink

Recommendations of where to stop for refreshment are given in these boxes. The numbers prior to each restaurant/café name link to references in the main text. Restaurants are also plotted on city maps.

Unless otherwise stated, restaurants are open daily for lunch and dinner. The $ signs at the end of each entry reflect the approximate cost of a meal for one person excluding taxes and drinks. These should be seen as a guide only. Price ranges, also quoted on the inside back flap for easy reference, are as follows:

$$$$	over B1,500
$$$	B700–1,500
$$	B200–700
$	below B200

Footers

Look here for the tour name, a map reference and the main attraction on the double page.

ARCHITECTURE

Explore Dusit's Thai-Euro grandeur (tour 5), the golden splendour of royal Rattanakosin (tour 1), towering spires and stupas at Wat Arun and Wat Pho (tour 2) or faded colonial architecture around Tha Oriental (tour 2).

RECOMMENDED TOURS FOR...

CHILDREN

Kids will love the animals and boating at Dusit Zoo (tour 5), the fish at Siam Ocean World (tour 7) and taking an express boat ride up the Chao Phraya River (tour 11).

ESCAPING THE CROWDS

Dip into Ko Kret's rural pace of life (tour 11) or the waterfall at Erawan National Park (tour 13); in town explore the quiet canals of Thonburi (tour 3).

HISTORY BUFFS

Marvel at the Chakri legacy of Rattanakosin (tour 1), the ancient capital Ayutthaya (tour 15), Old City temples (tour 4) and the eternal bustle of Chinatown (tour 6).

FOOD AND WINE

Be intoxicated by the steaming food stalls of Chinatown (tour 6), savour seafood by the seaside at Hua Hin and Pattaya (tours 17 and 18), or hunt out fusion flavours in Silom (tour 8).

NIGHT OWLS

Drink beers at backpacker bars in Banglamphu (tour 9), go go-go mad in Patpong (tour 8) or Pattaya (tour 18) or shop until late in Patpong Night Market (tour 8).

OUTDOOR ENTHUSIASTS

Trek in the jungle near Kanchanaburi (tour 13), cycle around compact Ko Kret (tour 11) or dive into some water sports off Pattaya's beaches (tour 18).

SHOPPERS

From Chatuchak's vast flea market (tour 10) to glitzy modern malls (tour 7) to Damnoen Saduak's traditional floating market (tour 12), Bangkok is a shopper's dream.

PARKS AND GARDENS

Stroll the manicured lawns of Dusit (tour 5), people-watch in Lumphini Park (tour 7) or go fly a kite in Sanam Luang (tour 1).

HANDS-ON CULTURE

Watch Thai kickboxing in action at Lumphini Stadium (tour 8), or learn the techniques from the masters at Sor Vorapin gym (tour 9), then heal your aches with a Thai massage course at Wat Pho (tour 2).

OVERVIEW

An overview of Bangkok's geography, customs and culture, plus illuminating background information on food and drink, shopping, nightlife and history.

CITY INTRODUCTION

Cosmopolitan Bangkok blends evocative street markets with glitzy modern malls, Buddhist philosophy with animism, and traditional reserve with lashings of sanuk (fun). The result is an effervescent milieu that draws visitors by the million.

Above: Thai dancer at Erawan Shrine; longtail boat.

When to Visit

The best time to visit Bangkok is during the cool season from late November to February, when temperatures range from 18–32°C (65–90°F), and it is less humid. The warm season is from March to mid-June, while the rains pour from June to October.

With an area of 1,565 sq km (604 sq miles), Bangkok is over 30 times larger than any other city in the kingdom of Thailand, and has a population of about 6 million (10–12 million in the greater metropolitan area). Although it is increasingly globalised and has readily adopted Western, Chinese and Japanese influences, the city remains steeped in its own rich culture and beliefs.

CITY OF ANGELS

Until the mid-18th century Bangkok was a duty port for tall ships bearing the world's cargoes, bound for the capital, Ayutthaya, 76km (48 miles) up-river. At the time it was a small but growing community called Bang Makok (Village of Wild Plums), although even by the 16th century it was already designated a town rather than a mere village. After the destruction of Ayutthaya, following a siege by the Burmese in 1767, the new king, Taksin, chose Thonburi, on the opposite river bank to Ban Makok, as his new capital.

Taksin was overthrown in 1782, and his successor King Rama I moved the capital across the river, digging canals to form the artificial island, Ko

Rattanakosin, which he planned in the image of Ayutthaya. After building the stunning Grand Palace, he chose an equally stunning name for his new city – Krungthepmahanakhon Amon-rattanakosin Mahintharayutthaya Mahadilokphop Nopphosin Ratcha-thaniburirom Udomrathaniwetmahasa Amonphiman Awatansathit Sakka-thatiya Witsanukamprasit, or 'City of Angels, Great City of Immortals, Magnificent City of the Nine Gems, Seat of the King, City of Royal Palaces, Home of the Gods Incarnate, Erected by Visvakarman at Indra's Behest'. It is the longest place name in the world. Thais call it Krung Thep (City of Angels), for short, while foreigners stick close to the original settlement's centuries-old name.

CITY LAYOUT

The low-lying capital grew slowly; it was a city of canals and elephant paths, with communities dwelling outside the old walls of Rattanakosin in Phra Nakorn (the Old City) and along the river in Chinatown and Dusit. Rapid 20th-century expansion – particularly from the economic boom in the 1980s – has resulted in a population 10 times bigger than that during World War II;

today, one in every six Thais lives here. Modern Bangkok has no definitive city centre, with major business and shopping areas now occupying Pathumwan, Silom and Sukhumvit. Across the river, in parts of Thonburi, canals still thread through bucolic countryside, and life is far quieter.

Navigating the City

Bangkok has major daytime traffic problems, one reason being that many roads are built over old canals, so they are often narrow. Although a growing network of expressways has alleviated some of the city's major daytime traffic problems, it is better when possible to travel by either the overhead Skytrain or the underground MRT systems, both of which are being extended. That said, air-conditioned taxis are comfortable, metered and inexpensive by international standards. Tuk tuks are fun, but rarely cheaper than taxis, and you are exposed to traffic fumes. Buses cost just a few baht but have little English signage, so require patience and an adventurous spirit. A pleasant and airy alternative is to travel by river, either by express boat to major piers or by longtail boat along the canals.

Exploring on Foot

Walking is an adventure. The colourful streets give an insightful peek into everyday life as you pick your way through vendors selling all manner of goods from stalls, wheeled carts and blankets on the ground. The going is easier in the older parts of the city, but you will still be walking in the heat.

Make use of the many convenience stores and itinerant traders to buy water or fruit; the latter is ready-cut in a bag with a cocktail stick so it is easy to eat on the move. And take your time: there is a good reason why the local people walk so slowly.

Four tours in this book – Rattanakosin, The Old City, Wat Arun and Wat Pho, and Banglamphu – are in and around the original walled city. The edges of some tours are close to the edges of others, so it is easy to mix and match the attractions.

FAITH AND BELIEFS

The postcard images of Buddhist monks in saffron robes may be clichéd, but they accurately reflect the importance of religion in the country. Around 95 percent of the nation subscribes to

Brahman Beliefs

Many of the Thais' non-Buddhist beliefs are Brahman in origin, and even today Brahman priests officiate at major ceremonies. The Thai wedding ceremony is almost entirely Brahman, as are many funeral rites. Royal ceremonies, such as the Ploughing Ceremony in May, are presided over by Brahman priests.

Theravada Buddhism, and there are signs of its significance everywhere, from the white bar on the national flag to Buddha images in the workplace and monks collecting alms in the street. Most men will spend at least a few days in a monastery, often following a family death, and even the monarch is required to have been ordained at some time in his life.

But Thailand, historically located on trade routes between larger powers, has always been populated by crossroads communities. As such, the people have become adept at bending under foreign influence and adapting cultural traits to suit their own needs. While Buddhism – which arrived via India and Sri Lanka – became dominant, there are still strong echoes today of Brahman beliefs that emerged from the Khmer kingdom in the East. Many pilgrimage sites are dedicated to Hindu gods, including the famous Erawan Shrine, and temples happily mix Buddhist and Hindu deities.

Also significant are older beliefs in animism and supernaturalism. Fortune tellers are widely visited (even by politicians), important events are organised to fall on auspicious days, and people wear tattoos that they believe will ward off danger. Objects such as buildings and trees are thought to contain spirits that must be placated lest they become agitated and return to show their displeasure. Thus, many have a spirit house or shrine where people leave offerings of food and drink to keep their occupants comfortable. It is a complex mix of beliefs that informs a large part of Thailand's unique character.

Power Plays

Since the advent of constitutional monarchy in 1932, Bangkok has witnessed many power plays. Early incidents, in 1949 and 1951, saw the army and police fighting navy-led coup attempts. Three tragic incidents centred on Thammasat University and Democracy Monument, in 1973, 1976 and 1992, resulted in many deaths as the police, military and private 'militias' opened fire. But since 2008 a struggle has divided the whole country. The People's Alliance for Democracy (PAD) (with close ties to the military and traditional elite, and wearing yellow) and the United Front for Democracy Against Dictatorship (UDD) (supporters of deposed ex-prime minister Thaksin Shinawatra, wearing red) have at various times occupied Government House, Bangkok airports and the commercial district in attempts to topple successive governments. Many deaths have resulted and the struggle continues.

THE MONARCHY

Since 1932 Thailand has been a constitutional monarchy in which the king exercises little formal power. However, the monarchy is a highly visible institution and many people display a genuine love for King Bhumibol Adulyadej (Rama IX), who ascended the throne in 1948 and is the world's longest-reigning monarch. As well as being admired for charitable works, particularly his rural development projects, he is viewed as a moral beacon in a country where corruption is widespread. His subjects also look to him as a calming influence during recurring times of political tension and coups d'état. The king's image is seen widely

in homes, workplaces and official buildings, and when the national anthem is played in schools and public places, such as cinemas, people stand respectfully. Recently, Thais have taken to wearing yellow to honour the king, and in 2007, when he was photographed leaving hospital wearing a pink shirt, within hours pink shirts were selling in their thousands across the country.

The monarchy's position is further cemented by the crime of lese-majesty, which can lead to terms of imprisonment for criticising the king. It is a law most often invoked by business or political rivals, and has been used widely since 2005 by members of most factions in the political crisis surrounding former prime minister Thaksin Shinawatra.

BANGKOK'S PEOPLE

Bangkok, perhaps more than most capital cities, is unrepresentative of the rest of the country. Because it has developed so rapidly there is often a stark contrast between traditional and contemporary lifestyles, and commentators often claim that 'Thainess' and its inherent family values are breaking down in the face of globalisation. The increasingly educated and confident middle classes are blurring the lines of a conventionally hierarchical society, while the MTV generation has taken the fuel of Western and Japanese pop culture to build an ever more edgy creative energy. However, examples of traditional lifestyles thread tantalisingly through the modern landscape, often around markets and temples.

Cultural variations are brought to the capital by migrant workers from Isaan in the northeast; by the large Chinese community; and by Indians, many of whom grew rich after World War II, when they returned to find their stocks of cotton intact in the warehouses while the price had skyrocketed.

In the Name of Fun

Three concepts in the local psyche are significant in forming the Thais' relaxed attitude to life. *Jai yen* (cool heart) and *mai pen rai* (never mind) underpin the tolerance towards the capital's many fringe lifestyles. The third, *sanuk* (fun), requires that everything – work, play, tragedy – should have elements of fun, and always with lots of friends. It is this that makes Bangkok one of the world's most exhilarating cities.

Above from far left: young novice monks; worshippers at a Chinatown temple; floating markets are disappearing as roads supersede waterways.

Land of Smiles
It is often handy to keep this advertising slogan in mind. Thais lose respect for people who lose their temper. When confronted by frustrations you will get far better results by smiling through it than by raising your voice.

FOOD AND DRINK

Thai cuisine is not all about tongue-searing dishes. Although the spiciness is initially overwhelming, what is most impressive is the complex balance of flavours that lies underneath.

Hot, Hot, Hot!
The small but very fiery Thai chillies *(prik)* come in red or green forms – both pack a potent punch. When sliced and served in fish sauce *(nam pla)* as a condiment, they are called *prik nam pla*.

Thai food is not just out-and-out spicy; most meals will include a number of less aggressive dishes, some subtly flavoured only with herbs, and northern cuisine in particular is characterised by milder flavours.

REGIONAL CUISINES

The variations of food and cooking styles are immense, as each of the country's four regions has a distinct cuisine of its own. The northeast is influenced by Laos, the south by Malaysia and Indonesia, the central area by the royal kitchens, and the north by Burma and Yunnan.

Northern Cuisine
This is the mildest of Thai cuisines. Northerners generally eat *khao nio* (sticky rice), kneading it into a ball to dip into sauces and curries such as the Burmese *kaeng hanglay*, a sweet and tamarind-sour pork dish.

Other northern Thai specialities include sausages, such as the spicy pork *sai oua* (roasted over a coconut-husk fire to impart aroma and flavour) and *naem* (fermented raw pork and pork skin seasoned with garlic and chilli). *Laab* is a salad dish of minced pork, chicken, beef or fish served with mint leaves and raw vegetables.

Thai Rice
Rice is the staple; in the past it sustained workers throughout the day with just small portions of chilli, curry or sauce added for flavour. Even now, rural Thais eat large helpings with just morsels of dried or salted fish. Thankfully, jasmine-scented Thai rice is one of the most delicious in Asia.

Dipping sauces include *nam prik ong* (minced pork, mild chillies, tomatoes, garlic and shrimp paste) and the potent *nam prik noom* (grilled chillies, onions and garlic). Both are eaten with the popular snack called *khaep moo* (crispy pork rind).

Northeastern Cuisine
Isaan food from the northeast is simple, generally spicy and eaten with sticky rice kept in bamboo baskets. Dishes include *som tam* (shredded green papaya, garlic, chillies, lime juice, and variations of tomatoes, dried shrimp, preserved crab and fermented fish) and a version of *laab* that is spicier and sourer than the northern version.

The most popular Isaan dish is perhaps *gai yang*, chicken grilled in a marinade of peppercorns, garlic, fish sauce, coriander and palm sugar, and served with both hot and sweet dipping sauces.

Southern Cuisine
The south, notable for Thailand's hottest dishes, also has gentler specialities such as *khao yam*, an innocuous salad of rice, vegetables, pounded dried fish and fish sauce. Slightly spicier are *phad sataw*, a stir-fry usually made with pork or shrimp, and *sataw*, a large lima bean lookalike with a strong flavour and

aroma. *Khao moke gai* is roasted chicken with turmeric-seasoned rice, often sprinkled with crispy fried onions.

Spicy dishes include *kaeng tai plaa*; fishermen who needed food that would last for days at sea are said to have created it by blending the fermented stomachs of fish with chillies, bamboo shoots and vegetables together with an intensely hot sauce. Even hotter is *kaeng leuang* (yellow curry), a variant of the central Thai *kaeng som*, with fish, green papaya and bamboo shoots or palm hearts in an explosive sauce.

Central Cuisine

Central cuisine, which has been influenced by the royal kitchens, includes many of the dishes made internationally famous at Thai restaurants abroad. It is notable for the use of coconut milk, which mellows the chilli heat. Trademark dishes include *tom kha gai*, a soup of chicken, coconut milk and galangal, the celebrated hot-and-sour shrimp soup *tom yum goong*, and *kaeng khio waan* (green curry), with chicken or beef, basil leaves and green aubergines. The intricate fruit and vegetable carvings seen at fine Thai restaurants are also a legacy of royal Thai cuisine. Stir-fries and noodle dishes are everywhere, due to the large Chinese presence in the central region.

COMMON DISHES

Kaeng

Usually translated as curry, *kaeng* covers a broad range, from thin soups to near-dry dishes like the northern

kaeng ho. Many *kaeng* are made with coconut cream, like the spicy red curry *(kaeng pet)* and *kaeng mussaman*, a rich, sweetish dish of Persian origin with meat, potatoes and onions.

Fish

Fish and seafood have featured prominently in Thai cooking since ancient times. *Haw mok talay* is mixed seafood in a curried coconut custard and steamed in a banana-leaf cup or coconut shell. Other delicious choices

Royal Thai Cuisine

The Grand Palace had many residences where each princess cooked what was called *ahaan chawang* (food for the palace people). These recipes spread through the wealthy classes via palace finishing schools and publications such as *Mae Krua Hua Baak*, the country's first cookbook, written by Thanpuying Pliang Pasonakorn, a descendant of King Rama II. The royal influence also spread to the wider populace through kitchen hands who had learned the recipes and started cooking them at home. A number of Thai restaurants connected to royalty began to open from the 1980s, but few authentic ones remain today. The intricate fruit and vegetable carving seen at fine Thai restaurants – such as the Sala Rim Naam at the Oriental Hotel – is also a legacy of Royal Thai cuisine.

Above from left:
trays of food at
Chatuchak Market;
Sirocco is the world's
highest al fresco
restaurant with
breathtaking views of
the city and the river
(see p.120).

to try are *poo pat pong karee* (steamed
chunks of crab in an egg-thickened
curry sauce with crunchy spring onion)
and *hoi malaeng poo op maw din* (mus-
sels in their shells, steamed in a clay
pot with lime juice and aromatic herbs).

Meat

Meat – usually chicken, pork or beef
– is cooked in all manner of styles, such
as pork fried with garlic and black
pepper *(muu thawd kratiam prik Thai)*
or the sweet-and-sour *muu pad prio
waan*, probably of Portuguese origin,
brought to Thailand by Chinese
immigrants. *Neua pad nam man hoi* is
a mild, delicate dish of beef, fried with
oyster sauce, spring onions and mushrooms. The popular and very spicy *pat
pet pat bai kaprao* dishes include meat
stir-fried with chillies, garlic, onions
and holy basil *(bai kaprao)*.

Below: *paad thai*
garnishes.

Noodles and Rice

Bangkok's ubiquitous street-side noodle
shops sell two types of noodles: *kuay
tiaw*, made from rice flour, and *ba mee*,
from wheat flour. Both can be ordered
broad *(sen yai)*, narrow *(sen lek)* or very
narrow *(sen mee)*, and with broth *(sai
naam)* or without *(haeng)*.

Common dishes are *kuay tiaw raad
naa* (rice noodles flash-fried and
topped with sliced meat and greens in
a thick, mild sauce) and *paad thai*
(narrow pan-fried rice noodles with
egg, dried and fresh shrimp, spring
onions, tofu, crushed peanuts and bean
sprouts). In *mee krawp* the rice noodles
are fried until crispy, tossed in sweet-
and-sour sauce and topped with sliced
chillies, pickled garlic and slivers of
orange rind.

FOREIGN INFLUENCES

There have been foreign influences in
Thai food for centuries. Even chilli is
a Portuguese import.

Fusion

Recent years have seen the growth of
a dedicated style of Thai-fusion dishes.
It often takes the form of Italian-Thai
blends, such as Thai-style spaghetti
with anchovies and chilli, served at
modern cafés like Greyhound, which
has several branches around the city.

Other modern Thai restaurants use
non-traditional ingredients like lamb
and salmon, and serve their essentially
Thai dishes Western-style. Common
among fusion items at several restaurants around town are salmon *laab*,

lamb massaman and foie gras with tamarind, of which there is an excellent version at Long Table. Many international restaurants – notably Bed Supperclub *(see p.117)* – also incorporate Thai flavours such as lemongrass and galangal into their East-West menus.

International Cuisine

But Bangkok offers far more than Thai food: it is fast emerging as an international culinary hotspot with options that include Japanese, Mexican, Italian and Spanish restaurants, and even a branch of a hip Michelin-starred French restaurant, D'Sens. The modern Indian Gaggan uses molecular techniques the chef learnt while working at El Bulli, in Spain *(see pp.116–21)*.

Thai-Chinese

Many ethnic Chinese in Thailand still speak the Teochew dialect of their southern Chinese ancestry, and most Chinese restaurants serve Teochew or Cantonese food. Especially famous are goose feet cooked in soy sauce, Peking duck, a wide variety of steamed and fried fish dishes, and the bite-sized lunch time snacks called dim sum. Poultry, pork, seafood and mushrooms are ubiquitous items along with noodles or rice, while piping-hot Chinese tea is an integral part of every meal.

DESSERTS

In Bangkok *khanom* (desserts) come in a bewildering variety, from light concoctions with crushed ice and syrup,

to custards, ice creams and little cakes, and an entire category based on egg yolks cooked in flower-scented syrups.

Generally light and elegant popular treats include *kluay buat chee* (banana slices in sweetened and salted warm coconut cream) and *kluay kaek* (bananas sliced lengthwise, dipped in coconut cream and rice flour, and deep-fried until crisp). Another favourite is *taap tim krawp* (water chestnut pieces covered in red-dyed tapioca flour and served in coconut cream and crushed ice), and *sangkhaya ma-praoawn*, a coconut cream custard steamed in a young coconut or a small pumpkin.

Look out for market vendors who sell 'rooftile cookies' *(khanom beuang)*, crispy shells filled with strands of egg yolk cooked in syrup with shredded coconut, sweet and spicy dried shrimp, coriander and coconut cream. And don't miss the heavenly *khao niao mamuand* (mango with sticky rice and coconut cream).

REFRESHMENTS

Thais drink locally brewed beers such as Singha, Kloster and the stronger Beer Chang. Foreign brands brewed on licence include Heineken. The middle-class obsession with French wines is waning, and there is now a decent selection available from the New World. Rice whisky brands Maekhong and Saeng Thip are popular, usually served with ice, soda and lime. Note that fresh fruit and ice drinks often get a splash of syrup (and salt) unless you request otherwise.

Coffee or Tea?
Thailand has its own special coffee made with a thick black mélange of coffee, tamarind and heaps of sweetened condensed milk. It is strong enough to set a dead person's heart palpitating. Thai iced tea is an orange-coloured concoction usually served with lashings of condensed milk.

Below: local diner.

SHOPPING

Bangkok is a retail destination for both spendthrifts and penny-pinchers. If you know where to look, just about anything is available, from traditional Thai pottery and handwoven silks to funky streetwear and designer goods.

Bargaining

Don't start bargaining unless you really want to buy. First, ask the price of the item. Then ask for a lower price. The seller will then lower the original price, thus signalling he or she is open to offers. Then offer your own first price, which should be too low. From there the bargaining begins until a final price is agreed.

Below: Thai craftsmen are adept at fashioning lacquerware; jewellery boxes embedded with coloured stones.

In Bangkok you can sniff out an antique under the awnings of an outdoor market or pick up a Hermès handbag from a glitzy luxury mall. While imported items are expensive, you will find locally produced wares incredibly affordable. And with most shops, malls and markets open daily from morning until night, you can easily shop 'til you drop.

TRADITIONAL PRODUCTS

Teakwood carvings come in the form of practical items such as breadboards and salad bowls, as well as more decorative trivets and statues of mythical gods, angels and elephants. Bronze statues of classical drama figures, like the recumbent deer from the *Ramakien* (the Thai version of the Indian classic fable the *Ramayana; see p.23*), make elegant decorations. Natural fibres woven into place mats, baskets and handbags also make great buys.

Lacquerware

Thai craftsmen excel at lacquerware, which is the art of overlaying wooden or bamboo items with glossy black lacquer, then adding artistic images painted in gold leaf. They are also supremely skilled at setting oyster shells in black lacquer backgrounds to create scenes of enchanting beauty.

Ceramics

Thais have been crafting pottery with great finesse for over 5,000 years. While original antiques are rarities, most ceramics are still thrown along the same shapes and designs of their age-old counterparts. Among the best known are Sangkhalok ceramic plates from ancient Sukhothai, most notably with distinctive twin-fish design.

Celadon is a beautiful stoneware with a light jade-green or dark-brown glaze, and is used to make dinnerware, lamps and statuary.

Benjarong originated in China and was later developed by Thai artists. Its name describes its look: *benja* is Sanskrit for 'five', and *rong* means 'colour'. The five colours of Benjarong – red, blue, yellow, green and white – appear on delicate porcelain bowls, containers and decorative items.

Popular blue-and-white porcelain, which also originated in China, has been produced extensively in Thailand for centuries.

ANTIQUES

Thai and Burmese antiques are among the finest in Asia, but the real thing is rare nowadays. For the tenacious and well informed, though, treasures can still be unearthed. The centre of the

city's antiques trade is River City (www.rivercity.co.th), with an array of shops selling genuine antiques and lookalike objets d'art. Note that the authorities maintain strict control over the export of religious antiques; dealers are usually able to clear buyers' purchases by obtaining export permits and shipping them abroad.

GEMS AND JEWELLERY

Thailand mines its own rubies and sapphires around the east-coast city of Chantaburi, and also sells stones from Burma and Cambodia. Rubies range from pale to deep red (including the famous 'pigeon's blood' red); sapphires come in blue, green and yellow, as well as in the form most associated with Thailand – the star sapphire. Thai jewellers can turn gold, white gold, silver and platinum into delicate jewellery settings and are able to produce both traditional and modern designs.

Be careful when shopping for gems and jewellery. One of Bangkok's most infamous scams involves touts telling tourists that a famous landmark, such as the Grand Palace, is closed and suggesting an alternative sight, a detour that often leads to a bogus gem deal. Buy only from reputable shops endorsed by the Tourism Authority of Thailand and the Thai Gem and Jewellery Traders Association. These shops carry the Jewel Fest (www.jewelfest.com) logo and issue a certificate of authenticity that comes with a money-back guarantee.

WHERE TO SHOP

Malls

The main shopping areas converge around Thanon Rama I and Thanon Ploenchit and are linked by a covered raised walkway, which means you can walk from mall to mall without ever touching terra firma.

Just a stone's throw from Siam Square *(see p.58)*, a warren of market stalls and shops catering to a trendy teenage clientele, is the high-end Siam Discovery Centre, as well as Mah Boon Krong (MBK), a multistorey bargain-hunter's heaven. Nearby is the gargantuan Siam Paragon mall, peppered with high-end boutiques, cafés, and even a Ferrari showroom. Further down the road is the even bigger Central World mall.

And there are plenty of luxury shops too, such as those at Gaysorn Plaza and Erawan Bangkok (both on Thanon Ploenchit near the Erawan Shrine). The latter has funky fashion from the likes of Galliano and Yamamoto.

Markets

Reputed to be the world's biggest flea market, with some 10,000 stalls, Chatuchak Weekend Market *(see pp.68–70)* is a must. The sheer variety of goods available is astounding. Patpong Night Market *(see p.63)*, in the city's red light district, has clothes, watches, CDs and DVDs, among other stuff, much of it of dodgy origin. Also worth an early morning visit is the Damnoen Saduak Floating Market *(see p.76)*.

Above from far left: Thai silk is available in many colours; Siam Square; Gaysorn Plaza is good for designer fashions; quirky souvenirs.

Save Money
Every June–July and December–January, major department stores and malls take part in the Thailand Grand Sales, although many also offer a 5 percent tourist discount year round – simply show your passport at the point of purchase. You can also claim a 7 percent VAT discount at the airport if your total purchases are worth B5,000 or more.

Below: wooden carving of a scene from the *Ramakien*.

NIGHTLIFE

Many visitors' expectations of Bangkok nightlife extend no further than the much-hyped Patpong go-go bars. They may be surprised to find ping-pong balls play only a small part in a thriving, cosmopolitan entertainment scene.

Safety

Bangkok is generally very safe for tourists, but exercising some caution is wise around red-light areas. Patpong bars, particularly upstairs, have been known to present rip-off bills and issue threats if you protest. It is best to pay, get a receipt, and take it to the Tourist Police at the head of the *soi* (street). Don't carry too much money in red-light bars and don't be flash with it.

Bangkok's nightlife ranks among the best in the world. The Thai affinity for *sanuk* (fun) sees bars and clubs offering everything from blues, house and hip hop to catwalks, clowns and art shows, often all on the same street. There is an increasingly vibrant indie scene, luxury hotels have jazzy cocktail lounges, and barn-like bars supply a variety of Thai-style country rock.

NIGHTLIFE ZONES

Bangkok has three designated nightlife zones: Thanon Silom, Thanon Ratchadaphisek and Royal City Avenue (RCA), in which venues with valid dance licences can stay open until 2am. The rest must (or should) close at 1am. The reality depends on the political and police agendas of the day. Bribery is rampant, and often these hours are flexible. Following a spate of police raids in the early 2000s, designed to curb drugs and under-age drinking, nearly all clubs now require you to show ID to gain entry, whatever your age.

The Silom zone includes the Patpong red-light district as well as numerous pubs and restaurants, but few dance clubs outside Soi 2 and Soi 4. Thanon Ratchadaphisek has some huge clubs and even larger massage parlours, visited mainly by Thais and

Asian tourists, and a clutch of smaller bars that attract young Thais. Of the three zones, RCA has developed into the most focused club scene, with a bunch of hip venues.

Other vibrant, but unzoned, nightlife areas include the backpacker enclave around Khao San Road, which is also a hangout for twentysomething Thais, Sukhumvit, home to two of the city's most famous international clubs, Q Bar and Bed Bar *(see also pp.122–23)*, and Thonglor.

VENUES

Entry fees for clubs were almost unheard of a decade or so ago, but in order to keep out the riff-raff (particularly working girls) and keep the crowd chic, several spots now impose a cover charge, which usually includes a couple of drinks.

Nightclubs

Dance music in clubs runs a gamut from techno through hip-hop, deep house, jungle, Indian vibes and countless variations led by cutting-edge venues such as LED, Bed Bar and Club Culture. International DJs like Goldie, Tiesto, Carl Cox and Fat Boy Slim have Bangkok on their tour schedules, adding to an increasingly confident posse of

expat and local DJs, such as Dragon, Seed and Funky Gangster.

Live Music

Good live jazz and blues venues include The Living Room, Saxophone and Niu's on Silom; axe-hero rock appears at Mello Yello on RCA; and look out for promoters Mind the Gap, who take their indie bands to various venues around town. Brick Bar on Khao San Road stages rock, ska and reggae, while at the nearby Ad Here players turn up to jam in a place the size of a guitar case. Tawandaeng German Brewhouse has an impressive arty cabaret fusion with Thai and Western influences.

Bars

High-fliers can sip fine champagne and cocktails at the rooftop Sky Bar (with jazz) and Distil (New York lounge sounds), both of which offer scintillating views of the city, while 'Lo-sos' head for Cheap Charlie's – nothing more than a bar (no roof, no walls) – on Sukhumvit Soi 11. For Guinness and hearty grub, go to one of the many British pubs around Thanon Silom or Thanon Sukhumvit.

Gay Scene

The thriving and overtly gay scene is concentrated around Silom Sois 2 and 4, be it quiet drinking and dining at Sphinx, boozy cruising at Telephone or hard dance at DJ Station. Soi 2 is exclusively gay, while Soi 4 is more of a free-for-all with street-side tables hosting a party-vibe *(see p.63)*.

KATOEY CABARET

The world-famous transsexual *(katoey)* cabaret revues feature sequined artistes who have gone through various stages of sex-change surgery, performing saucy lip-synching song-and-dance routines. New Calypso Cabaret (tel: 0 2216 8937; www.calypsocabaret.com) at the Asia Hotel has shows twice nightly.

DANCE DRAMA

Classical masked dance theatre called *Khon* is staged at Sala Chalermkrung Theatre every weekend. The most acclaimed contemporary shows are at Thonburi's Patravadi Theatre *(see p.39)*, which blends traditional and contemporary elements, both in the main theatre and at a restaurant setting close to the river.

NIGHT-TIME SPORTS

Bangkok at night is not all booze and boogie. Sporty types go disco bowling – to music and flashing lights – at several alleys in the city, play a round of night golfing at Panya Indra (www. panyagolf.com), or race their friends at the indoor go-karting track on RCA.

Nobody who comes to Thailand should miss the frenzied Muay Thai kickboxing bouts accompanied by the wailing of traditional music, and animated betting on the outcome. Lumphini National Stadium *(see p.60)* remains the world mecca, but Dusit's Ratchadamnoen Stadium *(see p.45)* also has mainstream fighters.

Above from far left: jazz at Saxophone; international crowd at Q Bar; Calypso Cabaret at the Asia Hotel.

Thai Country Music
Luk thung (Child of the Rice Fields) and *Morlam* (Doctor of Rap) are Thai country-music forms, mostly heard on taxi drivers' radios and performed in large venues on the outskirts of town. Shows often include ornately costumed theatrics, while the audience, primarily of migrant labour from Isaan, celebrates with spicy food and copious amounts of rice-based whisky.

HISTORY: KEY DATES

Following a series of bloody wars, Bangkok became the capital of Thailand in the 19th century. The city has survived colonial intrigue, coups, counter-coups and financial ruin to become the thriving metropolis it is today.

EARLY HISTORY

Nation State
Although Sukhothai is regarded as Thailand's first capital, the country then was not so much a nation as a relatively small and loose affiliation of independent states. Diplomacy, wars and skirmishes to unite the disparate parts into the area now known as Thailand continued until the early 20th century.

3,500BC	Bronze Age culture thrives at Ban Chiang in what is now northeast Thailand.
800s–1200s	The Thai (or Tai) migrate from China into northern Thailand.
*c.***1279–98**	Fledgling state of Sukhothai, north of the area known as Syam, expands under King Ramkamhaeng into the beginnings of a nation.
1350	Ayutthaya supplants Sukhothai as the capital of the loosely formed, but growing, nation of Siam.
1767	Burmese armies destroy Ayutthaya. The new king, Taksin, makes his capital at Thonburi.
1782	Taksin executed. Chao Phraya Chakri (Rama I) establishes the Chakri dynasty and moves the capital across the river to Bangkok.

GROWTH OF SIAM

Royal Island
After he assumed the throne in 1782, King Rama I created an artificial island called Rattanakosin, which was modelled on Ayutthaya. He built the Grand Palace there as a royal abode and centre of administration. It was home to Thailand's monarchs until 1935.

1851–68	King Mongkut (Rama IV) reforms laws and sets his people on a course towards modernisation.
1868–1910	Through diplomacy with Western nations, King Chulalongkorn (Rama V) helps Siam remain the only Southeast Asian nation not colonised. His modernisation includes the abolition of slavery.
1910–25	King Vajiravudh (Rama VI) promotes 'nationhood', and launches the current Thai flag.

Right: a city canal in the late 19th century.

1925–35	The reign of King Prajadhipok (Rama VII) is ended by a 1932 coup, in which he 'ceases to rule but continues to reign'.
1935	Ananda Mahidol (Rama VIII) is named king.
1939	Siam is renamed Thailand.

MODERN THAILAND

1946–72	King Ananda dies mysteriously in 1946 and is succeeded by his younger brother, King Bhumibol Adulyadej (Rama IX). The 1950s sees many coups and military-backed governments.
1973–6	Many die in a civil uprising that topples Prime Minister Thanom Kittikachorn. A democratic government is elected. Military rule is re-established in 1976 after more demonstrations and civilian deaths.
1976–92	A progressively softer, military-backed government fosters an elected government in 1988. Coups, starting in 1991, lead to street demonstrations and casualties in 1992. A new Democrat Party government is elected under Chuan Leekpai.
1995–7	Successive governments, largely seen as weak and corrupt, end with an economic crash and currency devaluation in 1997.

21ST-CENTURY THAILAND

2001	Elections bring billionaire businessman Thaksin Shinawatra and his Thai Rak Thai (Thais Love Thais) party to power.
2006	Demonstrators with yellow shirts to show allegiance to the monarchy demonstrate against Thaksin. The army stages a bloodless coup.
2008	New elected government is believed to be Thaksin's puppet. Thaksin, found guilty of corruption, flees the country. 'Yellow Shirt' demonstrators occupy Government House and Suvarnabhumi Airport. The courts disband the ruling political party and Democrat Party leader Abhisit Vejjajiva becomes prime minister.
2009	Pro-Thaksin UDD protestors (Red Shirts) disrupt the ASEAN Summit in Pattaya; Songkran riots erupt in Bangkok; Yellow Shirt leader Sondhi Limthongkul is shot, but survives.
2010	Thousands of Red Shirt demonstrators occupy parts of Bangkok. clashing violently with the army on 10 April and 19 May.
2011	Skirmishes between Thai and Cambodian troops escalate over a disputed border area. In July, the Thaksin proxy Pheu Thai Party, led by his sister Yingluck, wins a landslide election victory. That same month, terrible floods inundate over a third of Thailand's provinces; nearly 400 people lose their lives.

Above from far left: European impression of 17th-century Ayutthaya; 1947 coronation of King Bhumibol Adulyadej.

Ramakien
At the heart of Thai literature is the *Ramakien*, the Thai version of the Indian *Ramayana*. The enduring story has found a home in the literature, dance and drama of many Asian countries. It tells of the god-king Rama and his beautiful wife, Sita, who is abducted by the demon king Totsakan. Rama sets off in pursuit, stymied by mammoth obstacles that test his mettle. After a long battle Totsakan is killed, Sita is rescued, and everyone lives happily ever after.

Below: snapshots of modern Bangkok.

WALKS AND TOURS

RATTANAKOSIN

This once fortified island is the heart of Old Bangkok, with its extraordinary Grand Palace, the largest museum collection in Southeast Asia, a shrine that holds the city's spirit, and street scenes little changed in a century.

DISTANCE 3.5km (2¼ miles)
TIME A full day
START/END Tha Chang
POINTS TO NOTE
Express boats only stop at certain piers *(see p.108)*. This is a long tour; be sure to set aside a couple of hours for the Grand Palace alone. Admission to it also includes access to Vimanmek Mansion *(see p.47)*. The tour is best tackled Wed–Fri if you want access to both the interior of the Grand Palace and the National Museum.

Access to Cash
There are ATM machines to the right at Tha Chang Market and more beside the ticket booth in the Grand Palace.

THA CHANG

Take an express boat to the pier called **Tha Chang**, which leads to a lovely little market square of 19th-century shophouses and food stalls. If you are hungry, you can eat in *raan aharn* (food shops) around the edge or under the frangipani trees, where old women in straw hats chew on *miang kham* – a snack of betel leaves filled with morsels like chopped shallots, dried shrimp and chilli. It is a scene that could be a century old. Alternatively, through a gate to the right is **Sor Tor Lor**, see ⑪①.

GRAND PALACE COMPLEX

Emerging from the square at the main road, in front of you is the white-walled **Grand Palace complex ❶** (Thanon Na Phra Lan; tel: 0 2222 8181; daily 8.30am–3.30pm; charge), housing Bangkok's two essential sites – the Grand Palace and Wat Phra Kaew – the former royal residence and the country's principal temple.

Cross the road and walk ahead along Thanon Na Phra Lan, where opposite is **Silpakorn University**, the country's premier art school *(see margin, right)*. After 100m/yds you reach the palace main gate, where a sign proclaims: 'Do Not Trust Wily Strangers'. Take the

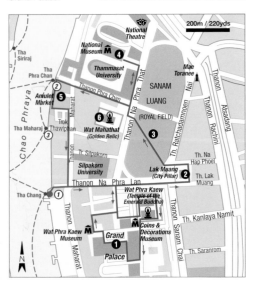

advice and ignore the touts hovering outside, who will tell you the palace is closed but they know the perfect alternative (this will end in a visit to a gem shop where the tout gets a commission), and follow the crowds towards the stunning gold and twinkling glass facades. It is forbidden to wear shorts, but you can hire trousers for a small fee.

Coins and Decorations

The ticket booth is 100m/yds ahead. Next to it is the **Coins and Decorations Museum Ⓐ**, with exhibits dating from the 11th century such as 'bullet coins', seals and ceramic coins in the downstairs rooms. Upstairs are displays of splendid royal regalia, including crowns, gem-encrusted swords and robes, plus decorations and medals made of gold and precious stones.

🛈 WAT PHRA KAEW

Beyond the museum is the stunning **Wat Phra Kaew Ⓑ** (Temple of the Emerald Buddha), which, as the king's personal chapel, has no resident monks. On the left as you enter, the gold mosaic **Phra Si Rattana Chedi** is said to enshrine a piece of the Buddha's breastbone. Next in line are the **Phra Mondop** (Library), which contains the *Tripitaka* (holy Buddhist scriptures) inscribed on palm leaves, and the **Prasat Phra Thep Bidom** (Royal Pantheon), surrounded by half-human, half-bird gilded bronze figures called *kinaree* (female) and *kinara* (male). It contains statues of the first eight Chakri kings.

Behind the Phra Mondop is a detailed sandstone model of the Khmer temple Angkor Wat, in Cambodia. Along its northern edge is the **Viharn Yot Ⓒ** (Prayer Hall) that is flanked on the left by the **Ho Phra Nak** (Royal Mausoleum) and **Ho Phra Montien Tham** (Auxiliary Library) on the right. Opposite Viharn Yot is the first of the wat's 178 murals that recount the *Ramakien*, the Thai version of the Indian epic the *Ramayana (see p.23)*.

Emerald Buddha

The main draw for Thai visitors to Wat Phra Kaew is the **Emerald Buddha**, which, despite standing a mere 66cm (26 inches) tall, is Thailand's most revered religious artefact. From the 15th century the statue was moved between monasteries in northern Thailand, then known as Lanna. In the 16th century Laotian King Chaichetta of Luang Prabang briefly ruled Lanna, and took the Emerald Buddha with him when he returned to his homeland. It remained in Laos until King Rama I (who before he ascended the throne was a celebrated general known as Chao Phraya Chakri), recaptured it from Vientiane in 1778.

Food and Drink 🍴

① **SOR TOR LOR**
Royal Navy Club, Tha Chang;
tel: 08 1257 5530; $
Part of the Royal Thai Navy Club but open to the public, this riverside operation is perched on a large wooden deck. It is recommended for fish and seafood standards like spicy steamed snapper with Thai lime, curried crab, and fried garlic prawns.

Above from far left: Grand Palace complex at dusk; the *bot* that enshrines the Emerald Buddha at Wat Phra Kaew.

Art on Show
Silpakorn University holds regular art shows, both by students and artists-in-residence. There is also an on-site bookshop with some titles about Thai art written in English.

Below: *yaksha* protector at Wat Phra Kaew; the revered Emerald Buddha.

Located in the *bot* (ordination hall), the Buddha, which is actually made of jade, not emerald, sits high on a golden throne, overseen by a nine-tiered umbrella and representations of the sun and moon. Kings Rama I and III made robes for the Buddha to wear, one for each season. They were replaced in 1996 to celebrate the current king's Golden Jubilee. He personally presides over robe-changing ceremonies: a golden, diamond-studded tunic for the hot season, a gilded robe flecked with blue for the rainy season, and one of enamel coated with solid gold for the cool.

GRAND PALACE

From Wat Phra Kaew, go south into the compound of the **Grand Palace** (building interiors closed Sat–Sun). Until the early 20th century this city within a city included kings' and kings' wives' quar-

ters, ceremonial buildings, military and civil wings, and a prison. Following the death of his brother King Rama VIII at the Grand Palace in 1946, the current king, Rama IX, moved to Chitralada Palace in Dusit *(see margin, p.46)*.

The buildings are roughly arranged in four clusters. On the left is the **Borombhiman Hall**, built in 1903, now used as a guesthouse for visiting heads of state, and behind it the **Buddha Ratana Starn** (Chapel of the Crystal Buddha). To the right is the **Phra Maha Montien Group**, which is dominated by three structures, opening with the **Amarin Vinitchai Throne Hall**. Built in 1785, this holds the royal throne, with its nine-tiered white canopy, and boat-shaped altar. Beyond this hall is the **Paisal Taksin Hall**, where new monarchs are crowned; and further back is the **Chakraphat Phiman Hall**, which was the royal residence for the first three

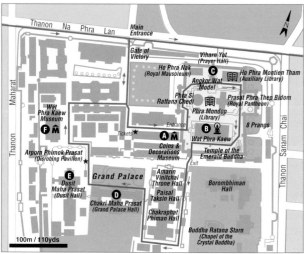

② Siwalai Gardens

Chakri kings. New monarchs still spend their first night here as a symbol of accession. The red poles topped by gold knobs located in the courtyard were once used to tether royal elephants.

Grand Palace Hall

The large building to the right of centre in the palace complex is the majestic **Chakri Maha Prasat ㊉**, the centrepiece of the Chakri Group. This Italianate structure, crowned with three spires on its Thai-style roof, was completed in 1882 to commemorate Bangkok's first centenary. The interior also blends Thai and Western features, a common practice during the reign of the much-travelled King Rama V (1868–1910).

Dusit Maha Prasat

To the right of this is the Dusit Group, which is centred around the **Dusit Maha Prasat ㊉**, a hall conceived by King Rama I as the place for his lying-in-state. He copied the exact dimensions of the Suriyamarin Throne Hall, which served the same purpose for the monarchs of Ayutthaya until its destruction in the 18th century. The Dusit Maha Prasat is still used as the final resting place of honoured royal family members before they are cremated in Sanam Luang *(see p.30)*. Also here is the exquisite **Arporn Phimok Prasat** (Disrobing Pavilion).

WAT PHRA KAEW MUSEUM

North of the Dusit Hall is the **Wat Phra Kaew Museum ㊉**, with its decorative lacquer screens and beautiful Buddha statues made of crystal, silver, ivory and gold. In the southern room on the second floor are two interesting scale models depicting the Grand Palace complex a century ago and as it looks today. A café to the right of the museum has lovely views from the veranda of the Dusit Maha Prasat.

LAK MUANG

Leave the complex via the main entrance and turn right until you reach a roundabout with a statue at its centre. Cross Thanon Sanam Chai and walk ahead to the white *prang* (Khmer-style tower) that holds the **Lak Muang ㊋** (City Pillar).

Thais believe everything, including trees and buildings, has a spirit; religious structures are often built over the ruins of old ones in order to protect the spirit of the old. The Lak Muang is Bangkok's

What's a Wat?
You will see wats, or Buddhist temples, everywhere in Bangkok. Other common architectural terms include: *bot* – the ordination hall of a temple, where religious rites are held; *viharn* – a replica of the *bot* that is used to keep Buddha images; *prang* – an ellipse-shaped stupa based on the corner tower of a Khmer temple and also housing images of the Buddha; and *chedi* (stupa) – the most venerated structure, a bell-like dome that originally enshrined relics of the Buddha, later of holy men and kings.

The Chakri Capital

When Rama I (Chao Phya Chakri), the first king of the Chakri dynasty, chose what is now known as Bangkok as the new capital in 1782, he attempted to build it in the image of the former capital, Ayutthaya, both as an aesthetic device and as a declaration of power. He dug canals and built walls – in some cases reusing stones from Ayutthaya – turning Rattanakosin into a fortified island *(ko)*. Hence the full name of this area is Ko Rattanakosin. The area around the Grand Palace was at the time occupied by Chinese traders, who were moved down river, becoming the early inhabitants of Chinatown *(see p.49)*. Some accounts record the king living modestly on the Grand Palace site during the three years it took to build. There were three days of celebrations when it was finished.

Below: National Museum; elephant-shaped topiary in the grounds; Buddhai-sawan Chapel.

foundation stone, and is believed to contain the spirit of the city itself. As such, it is seen as the point from which Bangkok's power emanates, and is the object of many people's prayers for favour in work, love or lottery winnings. The shrine contains two *lingam* (phallic columns associated with the Hindu god Shiva), the second one being the Lak Muang of Thonburi, which was moved here when the district (and former capital) became part of Bangkok. Also buried inside is the city's horoscope, as rewritten by King Rama IV (1851–68).

City Pillar Compound

On the other side of the entrance gate is a shrine holding statues of the city's five guardian spirits. Walk further into the compound; the nine Buddha figures on the right symbolise the days of the week, and night and day, each with a naked torch flame burning before it. People go to the combination that corresponds to their birth time and pour in bottles of oil, which represent life, to ensure long and happy days ahead. Opposite, devotees shake sticks from cups in yet another method of divining the future.

Near the gate at the end of the path, a **traditional theatre group** (daily 8.30am–4.30pm) performs scenes from the *Ramakien (see p.23)*, paid for by people whose wishes have been granted. Turn left at the gate into Thanon Na Hap Phoei.

SANAM LUANG

Recross the main road, enter the large park and walk through it diagonally to the opposite corner. This expanse is **Sanam Luang** ❸, where royal ceremonies and cremations are carried out. Prior to closing for renovations in 2011 it was a base for hawkers, fortune tellers and the homeless. Time will tell whether they will return. Each March the Thai Kite, Sport and Music Festival held here hosts fairground games, folk music and traditional sports. Previously, these grounds have been a racecourse, a golf course and home to a Sunday market; the market moved to Chatuchak in 1982 when Sanam Luang was being prepared for the Bangkok Bicentennial.

NATIONAL MUSEUM

Come out of the park, cross Thanon Na Phra That and turn right. Make your way past **Thammasat University**, Thailand's second most prestigious educational establishment (after Chulalongkorn University), to the adjacent **National Museum** ❹ (4 Thanon Na Phra That; tel: 0 2224 1333; www.thailandmuseum.com; Wed–Sun 9am–4pm; charge, guided tours available at 9.30am in English). Its collection, which is claimed to be the largest in Southeast Asia, and which was begun in 1874 with personal items belonging to King Rama IV, is displayed in three groups in buildings that were once the palace of the deputy king (an office that was phased out in 1870).

Buddhaisawan Chapel

The **Buddhaisawan Chapel**, to the right of the ticket office, is significant

for its beautiful murals and the bronze **Phra Buddha Sihing**, Thailand's second-most sacred religious image. The statue is paraded through the streets each year on the eve of Thai New Year, Songkran, the famous festival in which people playfully drench each other with water. Don't miss the **Walking Buddha**, whose pose is unique to Sukhothai art.

Historical Exhibits

Despite poor exhibit descriptions, the museum takes you on a fascinating journey into Thailand's past. Galleries include those showcasing ancient Ban Chiang pottery, theatre, and the arts of Ayutthaya, Sukhothai and Lanna, as well as displays including golden royal funeral chariots, puppets and textiles.

AMULET MARKET

Walk back along Thanon Na Phra That, take the first right into Thanon Phra Chan and then walk through the small market at the end leading to Tha Phra Chan. At the pier follow the left path into the **Amulet Market ❺** (daily 9am– 6pm), a busy warren of lanes where people bargain for all kinds of religious items, from large Buddhas to tiny carvings that you need a magnifying glass to inspect. The lane running from the pier is lined with hole-in-the-wall cafés, where you can grab something tasty to eat, see 🍴②. It leads eventually through Trok Wat Mahathat to Thanon Maharat. (Many of the lanes off it will also end here.)

WAT MAHATHAT

As you emerge from the market on Thanon Maharat, across the road is **Wat Mahathat ❻**, Thailand's first Buddhist university, whose name means Golden Relic. King Rama IV spent many years here as a monk before ascending the throne in 1851. It has the largest *bot* in Thailand, with room for 1,000 devotees, but the temple interior is closed to the public. The **International Buddhist Meditation Centre** here has classes available in English (tel: 0 2623 5881, ext. 1).

Heading south along Thanon Maharat, the next street on the right, Trok Thawiphan, has a sign saying Maharaj Pier. You can only catch expensive tourist boats from here, but there is a good place to eat: **S & P**, see 🍴③. Otherwise continue for 200m/yds to Tha Chang, where you can catch the express boat home.

Above: line of seated Buddha images at Wat Mahathat.

Future Forecast
Amulets are associated with fortune, both good and bad, so in the lanes around the Amulet Market you willl also find astrologers working in palmistry, Thai astrology and tarot. There are several more at Tha Phra Chan.

WAT ARUN & WAT PHO

This tour takes in two of Bangkok's most important temples, the famous Oriental Hotel and links to the early international trading communities that clustered around the Old Customs House in the 19th century.

DISTANCE 6.5km (4 miles)
TIME A half day
START Tha Tien pier
END Oriental Hotel
POINTS TO NOTE
This is an easy walk; the distance travelled is mostly by boat. If you like temples and cultural sites, it is straightforward to add the Grand Palace and Wat Phra Kaew (see pp.26–9) to the first part of the tour. They are just a 10-minute walk, turning right onto Thanon Maharat from Wat Pho.

Below: Wat Pho's main *chedi* are dedicated to Thailand's monarchs.

Explore this historic stretch of the Chao Phraya River by boat, stopping off to visit the best of what the southern part of Rattanakosin has to offer.

WAT ARUN

From Tha Tien, take the ferry across to **Wat Arun ❶** (34 Thanon Arun Amarin; tel: 0 2891 1149; www.watarun.org; daily 7.30am–5.30pm; charge). Also known as the Temple of Dawn, it is one of Bangkok's premier attractions. The confusing nickname – the sun actually sets, not rises, behind the temple – dates back to the time of King Taksin, who led the remnants of the Siamese armies here in 1767 after their defeat by the Burmese in the siege of Ayutthaya. The king first viewed Wat Arun at dawn, and chose the area, Thonburi, as the new capital of Siam.

Taksin incorporated the temple – at that time called Wat Magog – into his palace compound. He renamed it Wat Jaeng (The Temple of Dawn) and housed the greatly revered Emerald Buddha here. King Rama I later moved it to Wat Phra Kaew (see p.27), near the Grand Palace. Rama II (1809–24) officially changed the name to Wat Arunratchatharam, and Rama IV (1851–68) later chose the name Wat Arunratchawararam.

The Temple Today

After renovations by several of the Chakri kings, the main Khmer-style *prang* (spire) today stands at 79m (259ft). The four faces of the *prang* have statues depicting events in the Buddha's life and steep staircases offering pleasant views of the city. The main *prang* and four smaller ones in the courtyard are decorated with tiny porcelain shards shaped into flowers, a technique that arose in the Ayutthaya era using recycled pottery that had been smashed during merchant voyages from China. The trident of Shiva tops each *prang*. Other notable features include the 19th-century *bot* (ordination hall), in which the main Buddha statue contains relics of Rama II.

WAT PHO

Recross the river by ferry, walk past the entrance to Tha Tien Market and across Thanon Maharat to the entrance of **Wat Pho** ❷ (2 Thanon Sanam Chai; tel: 0 2222 5910; daily 8am–5pm; charge). There has been a temple on this site for around 400 years, making it Bangkok's oldest, and following several restorations and additions it is now also the biggest. Although the official name is Wat Phra Chetuphon, it is still popularly known by a derivative of its original name Wat Photharam.

Reclining Buddha

Of particular interest is the breathtaking **Reclining Buddha**, added to the site by Rama III (1824–51). The reclining pose depicts the Buddha

Above from far left: colourful boat; detail, Wat Arun; the temple's main *prang*.

Origin of the Species The figures of animals in the grounds of Wat Pho are made of reclaimed ballast from 18th-century rice ships.

Above from left:
Assumption Cathedral; Reclining Buddha at Wat Pho; riverside drinks at the Oriental Hotel.

River Books
The publisher River Books sells its excellent tomes on Thai culture from premises at 396/1 Thanon Maharat (tel: 0 2224 6686; www.riverbooksbk.com). The compound is owned by the daughter of Prince Chula Chakrabongse, a noted historian. It is still the family residence, and they rent out four tranquil river-front villas (www.thaivillas.com) that are among the best independent accommodation in the city (*see p.110*).

ascending into Nirvana, having reached enlightenment. The enormous dimensions of the gilded statue within a building seemingly far too small add to the sense of exaltation. At the far end of its 45m (147ft) length are 108 *laksana* (distinctive marks of a Buddha), rendered in intricate mother-of-pearl inlays on the soles of the feet.

Thai Massage

In the courtyard are statues of ascetics demonstrating physical exercises, and on the walls a series of lessons on history, literature and astrology. Another legacy of Rama III, they led to Wat Pho being known unofficially as the country's first 'university'. People still come here to learn meditation and traditional medicine, and Thai massage sessions are offered to the public for a small fee by trained practitioners.

MUSEUM OF SIAM

Leave Wat Pho by its eastern gate and then turn right. After 150m/yds, the

Museum of Siam ❸ (4 Thanon Sanam Chai; tel: 0 2622 2599; Tue–Sun 10am–6pm; charge) has inter-active multimedia displays and tableaux explaining what it means to be 'Thai'. It starts 2,000 years ago and runs through historical eras and various population shifts, including the periods of Khmer, Sukhothai and Ayutthayan dominance.

CHINESE SHOPHOUSES

Take Soi Setthakan, west of the museum, walk to Thanon Maharat and turn right. After 50m/yds, on the left begins an evocative row of shophouses very possibly owned by the descendants of Chinese traders who originally set up on these plots before Bangkok was the capital. In some cases, particularly the herbalists, they may even be selling the same range of goods. After 100m/yds, turn left down Soi Pratu Nokyung to a delightful restaurant with river views, called **The Deck**, see ①①.

RIVER ATTRACTIONS

After lunch, go back to Tha Tien and catch an express boat towards Saphan Taksin. After a few minutes you will pass the cream-and-pink **Santa Cruz Church ❹** on the right, which, although rebuilt several times, has been a place of worship for Portuguese settlers since the 17th century, an era when European missionaries, merchants and mercenaries all plied their trade along the Chao Phraya River up to Ayutthaya.

Food and Drink

① THE DECK
Arun Residence, 36–38 Soi Pratoo Nok Yoong; tel: 0 2221 9158; $$–$$$
The Deck dishes up Thai-Euro fusion fare, such as carpaccio of tea-smoked duck, against a cute backdrop, with outdoor seating, views of Wat Arun and a bar on the third floor.

② THE VERANDAH
Mandarin Oriental Bangkok, 48 Charoen Krung Soi 40; tel: 0 2659 9000; $$–$$$
Watch the boats from this smart riverside terrace while you grab a coffee and sandwich or dine on ceviche of silver bream, and delicious home-made ice cream. Smart-casual dress code after 6pm.

Further on are the black iron spans of **Memorial Bridge** ❺. Though the bridge wasn't built at the time, it was at a river crossing here that the mid-19th-century Scottish merchant Robert Hunter first saw the original Siamese twins, Chang and Eng, swimming near the bank. He arranged to send them to the US, where they appeared in P.T. Barnum's Circus.

Just after the Royal Orchid Sheraton, about 1km (²/₃ mile) further down river on the left, a green-and-red flag marks the **Portuguese Embassy** in its garden compound. When it opened in the early 19th century, it was the country's first embassy. Further on the left, the crumbling white colonial building housing fire engines is the Old Customs House *(see right)*.

AROUND THA ORIENTAL

Alight at Tha Oriental and stroll past food stalls and the sadly dilapidated Venetian-style buildings of the **East Asiatic Company** and the former **Chartered Bank**. Turn right under the archway after 50m/yds to enter a small square that contains **Assumption Cathedral** ❻ (23 Charoen Krung Soi 38; tel: 0 2234 8556; daily 6am–9pm; free). Its rococo interior incorporates an intricate altar, a high, domed ceiling and stained-glass windows.

Leave the cathedral, walk down the side of the building and turn left at Assumption College. At the end of this alley, note the beautiful carved wood roofs on the old shops opposite, and take the small *soi* beside them on the

left. At the top of this lane, opposite is **Haroon Mosque**, part of a Muslim community whose wooden houses have occupied this stretch of river since the early 19th century.

Turn left and walk 100m/yds to the entrance of the **Old Customs House**. This handsome though neglected building was known as the southern gate of the city in the 19th century. The current inhabitants are firemen, and no one seems to mind if you wander around a little.

Now go back the way you came, turn right at the French Embassy then left into **OP Place** ❼ (30/1 Charoen Krung Soi 38; tel: 0 2266 0186; daily 10am–7pm), which is billed as an Asian Heritage Shopping Centre.

Oriental Hotel

Turn left out of OP Place, then right on Soi 40, towards the river. On the right is the **Mandarin Oriental Bangkok** ❽ (48 Charoen Krung Soi 40; tel: 0 2659 9000), the city's oldest up-market accommodation *(see p.113)*, where rock stars might mingle with royalty in the jazz bar. The original seamen's rest house here burnt down in 1865, and was replaced by what is now known as the Author's Wing, four sublime period suites named after authors who have stayed here, and one – Joseph Conrad – who probably did not.

The ground floor has a lovely colonial-style tearoom, with black-and-white photos of old Siam on the walls. Finish the tour with a well-deserved coffee or snack at the river-front **Verandah**, see ⑪②.

First Road

The lanes around Tha Oriental branch off Thanon Charoen Krung, which was Thailand's first paved road when it was built in 1861. It ran through Chinatown *(see pp.49–54)*, turning this area into the principal location for international businesses. It is now full of gold, silver and antiques shops.

Below: Santa Cruz Church.

THONBURI

Take a boat ride along one of Bangkok's old canals to visit spectacular royal barges, the craftsmen of Ban Bu and a temple that was once an execution site. Then hit dry land for some gruesome forensic science at Siriraj Hospital and more savoury scenes at Siriraj Market.

DISTANCE 6.5km (4 miles)
TIME A half day
START Tha Chang
END Patravadi Theatre
POINTS TO NOTE

This tour is mostly done by boat. The simplest way to organise this is to hire one from tour operators at Tha Chang. The pier is a good starting point because it is near the mouth of Khlong Bangkok Noi. Hire one for two hours, which will cost around B1,500 (cheaper if you bargain) and comfortably seat eight people. Arrange the stops you want to make before you fix the price and get in.

Further Afield
Tour operators can advise on trips that travel deeper into the canals of Thonburi. You could even travel all the way to Damnoen Saduak this way *(see p.76)*.

Today, Thonburi, the former capital of Thailand, resembles cosmopolitan Bangkok's slightly old-fashioned relation. But this is a good thing, as its canals offer a glimpse of a fast-disappearing world in which most Bangkokians lived on water.

Elephant Pier
Tha Chang (Elephant Pier) is so called because in the 18th and 19th centuries the royal pachyderms were brought here from the Grand Palace to bathe.

Canal Life

The most common transport into the canals is the longtail boat, so named because it has an outboard motor on a 3m (10ft) pole angled into the water behind it. Sit towards the front for a

quieter ride, although even these powerhouses move slowly in the canals and are relatively quiet. It is an adventure in itself tootling past houses on stilts with steps down to the water. Originally, people would come down them to bathe and to pick up supplies from passing boats, which offered everything from food to a postal service. As you travel, small boats will pull alongside to offer you beer, bread or the energy drinks that are a staple of the Bangkok worker's diet.

A little way upriver from Tha Chang, the boat will turn left into **Khlong Bangkok Noi**.

ROYAL BARGE MUSEUM

You soon arrive at the **Royal Barge Museum ❶** (Thanon Arun Amarin; tel: 0 2424 0004; daily 9am–5pm; charge) on the right-hand side, which houses spectacular golden barges used on important royal occasions. Their last outing – to celebrate the king's 80th birthday in 2007 – saw 2,000 oarsmen, musicians and guards in traditional dress sailing in a procession of 52 barges to Wat Arun for a *khatin* ceremony, in which robes are presented to monks. Of the six barges displayed in dry dock here, pride of place goes

to *Suphannahongse* (Golden Swan), named after the mythical steed of the Hindu god Brahma. The king travels in it on a gold-coloured throne. At 50m (164ft) long, it is the largest vessel in the world to be crafted from a single piece of wood. Barge processions date to the Ayutthaya period, but the original *Suphannahongse* was built in the reign of King Rama I (1782–1809). King Rama VI launched the current one in 1911.

Also on display are old figureheads from boats damaged by World War II Allied bombs aimed at the nearby Bangkok Noi Railway Station, which was used by the Japanese to ship supplies to and from western Thailand and the infamous Death Railway to Burma *(see p. 78).* Around the museum are glass cases with models of traditional canal transport, Ayutthaya-era drawings, photos of barge construction, and gold ornamental cloths that are used to adorn the barges.

BAN BU VILLAGE

A few minutes by boat from the museum, there is a small landing on the left with stone steps and a short alley leading to the market community of **Ban Bu** ❷. The craftsmen here make bronze-ware bowls called *khan long hin*. They are the descendants of settlers who fled Ayutthaya after it was destroyed by the Burmese in 1767. The village originally centred on small factory workshops that hired all the other families to do piecework from their own houses. Today **Jiam**

Sangsajja (Charan Sanit Wong Soi 32; tel: 0 2424 1689; Mon–Fri 9am–5pm) is the only remaining factory. To find it, go left at the market, and after 70m/yds turn right into a gate in an unmarked brown fence (you should hear the hammering). They still make bowls largely in the traditional way by

Above from far left:
Suphannahongse and
Narai Song Suban
barges; craftsman's
forge at Ban Bu;
canalside dwellings.

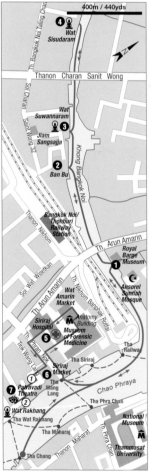

Weekend Extra
If you travel along
Khlong Bangkok Noi
on Saturday or
Sunday you can also
visit Taling Chan
Floating Market and
see weekend trading
as it used to be on
the canals. Just ask
at the pier to add it to
your itinerary.

Niche Museums
Siriraj Hospital
includes a Museum
of Thai Medicine
with displays about
traditional practices
such as the use
of herbs and Thai
massage. The
Forensic Museum
contains the skeleton
of its founder, Dr
Songkran Niyomsane.

hand-beating bronze into various shapes and stone-polishing the bowls to a beautiful, deep lustre. You can watch all the processes from smelting to polishing. Traditionally, *khan* were used to keep drinking water cool and to carry food to give as alms to monks, who also used them. People now use machine-made *khan*, and most bowls made here are sold as decorative items (B700–10,000), which is why they have engraved designs, something that was not part of the original process.

WAT SUWANNARAM

The next stop is **Wat Suwannaram ❸** (33 Charan Sanit Wong Soi 32; tel: 0 2434 7790/1; daily 5am–9pm; free). This is a delightful temple, and because it is off the beaten track you may find yourself the only person there. It was founded in the Ayutthaya period as Wat Thong, and in the reign of King Taksin (1767–82) became the execution site for Burmese prisoners of war held at the nearby Bang Kaew Camp.

It was restored in the reign of King Rama I (1782–1809) and renamed Wat Suwannaram. Further restorations during the reign of King Rama III (1824–51) included murals in the *ubosot* (chapel) painted by contemporary master artists Thongyu and Kongpae, which are now the only surviving examples of their work. From the reigns of Rama III to Rama V the temple was used as a cremation ground for the royal family and high-ranking officials.

Below: at prayer.

WAT SISUDARAM

A short way further up the canal, past verandas bright with orchids in hanging baskets, is **Wat Sisudaram ❹** (Soi Sisudaram; tel: 0 2882 5648; daily 6am–8pm; free). From its pier, go right past the Chinese pagoda, where a man sells bread to feed fish called *pla sawai* which, in their hundreds, thrash around in anticipation in the canal.

A few metres further, turn left. There is a massage shop on the left and, opposite, a huge golden statue of **Phra Somdej Toh**, former abbot of Wat Rakang, located near the Patravadi Theatre *(see right)*. Before the statue are Buddhist and Hindu deities, and behind it, facing the river, a small shrine to Thailand's greatest poet, Sunthorn Phu (1786–1855), who studied here. The red-painted wooden building across the courtyard from the massage shop is **Sala Kanparian**, a structure that dates from the Ayutthaya period and originally stood on stilts. The ground floor has now been built up with concrete.

SIRIRAJ HOSPITAL

On the way back, ask the boatman to drop you off at Tha Wang Lang, also called Phran Nok, and walk from the pier straight into Thanon Phran Nok. After 50m/yds go through the gates of **Siriraj Hospital ❺** (Thanon Phran Nok; tel: 0 2419 7000; museums: Mon–Sat 9am–4.30pm; charge) on the right. King Rama V founded the hospital in 1888, and named it after one of his sons who had died of

Above from far left:
Wat Suwannaram;
Buddhist and Hindu
deities at Wat
Sisudaram; golden
statue of Phra
Somdej Toh.

cholera. It was Thailand's first hospital and medical school and now contains several small museums *(see margin, left)* of exhibits used in lectures.

From the road walk 200m/yds and turn left at the **Anatomy Building**, where the first museums are situated. After this block turn right then left almost at the end. If you have a sturdy constitution, enter the **Adulyadej-vikrom Building**, where photos of dead bodies labelled 'Multiple Stab Wounds', 'Train Accident' and 'Blast Force: Hand Grenade', as well as displays about the 2004 tsunami, malaria, scabies and blood flukes, leave nothing to the imagination.

SIRIRAJ MARKET

Turn left from the Adulyadejvikrom Building and left again. After 200m/yds you are back on Thanon Phran Nok. Cross the road, turn left, and after 30m/yds turn into the alley on the right next to the chemist. Turn left at the top into Trok Wang Lang, the heart of **Siriraj Market** ❻. Amid the clothes and general goods, this place is especially good for food, from huge plastic bags stuffed with sweets and dried fruits to carts offering varieties of the intense *nam phrik* dipping sauces that are among Thailand's favourite condiment. On the right next to a sign saying 'Wienna' is *somtam* seller **Pa Sidaa**, see ⑪①.

At the end of the lane, turn right, walk to the last junction, then go left and right to find the **Patravadi Theatre** ❼ (69/1 Soi Wat Rakhang; tel: 0 2412 7287; www.patravaditheatre.com). Here

Patravadi Mejudhon, the city's best-known fringe director, stages traditional and contemporary dance drama. She also owns **Studio 9**, see ⑪②, which offers mainly Thai food, in a riverside setting. From here turn right, then left and right again. Follow the lane to the end, and take an express boat from Wang Lang to return to the city.

Food and Drink

① PA SIDAA
112/5 Trok Wang Lang; tel: 0 2412 7189; daily 9am–7pm (closed every other Sun); $
Serves grilled meats and Thai salads, but is famous for *somtam*, the fiery sour salad of green papaya laced with lime juice and chilli. It offers 11 versions, including the pungent Isaan original, with crushed black crabs and raw fermented sauce.

② STUDIO 9
69/1 Soi Wat Rakang; tel: 0 2866 2144; daily 11am–10pm; $$
A beautiful riverside setting for dishes like paprika chicken with rice, and spare ribs in pepper and garlic, accompanied by dance performances (Sat–Sun). Cheaper meals are available in the theatre café opposite.

History of Thonburi

Nearly 500 years ago the Chao Phraya River followed a long loop through what is now Thonburi. In 1542 King Chairacha ordered a canal to be dug to cut off the loop and shorten the route to the capital, Ayutthaya. Over the next 200 years the new canal widened through use and the effects of monsoon flooding until it became part of the river. The old loop was redesignated as two *khlongs* (canals) now called Bangkok Noi and Bangkok Yai.

Bangkok, then called Bang Makok (Village of Wild Plums), was effectively cut in two by the new river course. As a fort had already been built on the western bank near Wat Arun *(see p.32)*, when King Taksin (1767–82) came to power after the fall of Ayutthaya to the Burmese, he chose Thonburi as the new capital of Thailand.

THE OLD CITY

Soak up the atmosphere of early Bangkok in lanes containing some of the capital's most important temples. For 200 years monks have shopped here for amulets, Buddha images and powerful phallic symbols.

Ghosts' Gate

In the 19th century the dead of poor families were taken through the *Pratu Phi* (Ghosts' Gate) to Wat Saket to be cremated. During a bad cholera outbreak in 1849, when 20,000 people died in one month, resources were so stretched that corpses had to be left lying on the cemetery ground. This soon attracted hungry vultures and dogs.

DISTANCE 4km (2½ miles)

TIME 5 hours

START Loha Prasat, Wat Ratchanatda

END Phra Buddha Yodfa Monument

POINTS TO NOTE

To get to Wat Ratchanatda from downtown, take either a taxi or a river taxi along Klong Saen Saeb from Pratunam Pier. Tell the conductor you are going to Tha Saphan Pan Fah. The time given above does not include meal stops.

Right: golden *chedi* atop Golden Mount.

Together with the area covered in the Rattanakosin tour, this part of the city comprises the spiritual and historical heart of Bangkok; numerous temples and shrines are located here.

LOHA PRASAT AND WAT RATCHANATDA

Begin the tour at the **Loha Prasat** ❶ (Metal Palace; 2 Thanon Maha Chai; tel: 0 2224 8807; daily 9am–5pm; charge), which is the most striking element of the **Wat Ratchanatda** temple complex. Rama III (1824–51) ordered the step pyramid-style construction in 1846, to be modelled on a Sri Lankan temple from the 3rd century BC. Its 37 black metal spires, each topped with an umbrella-like embellishment called a *hti*, represent the virtues needed to attain Buddhist enlightenment.

You can climb a spiral staircase past corridors of meditation cells right onto the roof itself, where a tower holds a sacred bell. Dizzying views include the Golden Mount *(see right)*.

In the wat forecourt, to the left as you enter from Thanon Maha Chai, monks wander around the **Wat Ratchanatda Buddha Centre**, a small market that specialises in prayer beads, Buddha images, amulets and pennants bearing the faces of revered monks.

Inside, at the back, a tiny stall has a selection of wooden *palad khik* (phalluses), which are believed to ward off evil spirits. Many will have been blessed by monks for use in exorcism.

WAT SAKET AND THE GOLDEN MOUNT

Come out of the wat onto Thanon Maha Chai and turn left. At the traffic lights turn right, go past the remaining walls of **Mahakan Fort**, part of the original city ramparts, and across the bridge. Turn right and cross the next bridge. A short way along on the left is **Wat Saket** (344 Thanon Chakkaphatdi Phong; tel: 0 2223 4561; daily 8am–5pm; free) and the **Golden Mount ❷** (daily 7.30am–5.30pm; charge).

This is the site of the former Wat Sakae, where King Rama I stayed and was blessed on his way to Thonburi to assume the throne in 1782. He later restored the temple and renamed it Wat Saket. Low-lying Bangkok got its then highest vantage point in 1865 when Rama IV completed the 78m (256ft) high Golden Mount, so called because it is topped with a golden *chedi*.

Take the gentle climb past rock gardens with ringing temple bells and a 360-degree view of the city as the path spirals upwards. There's a refreshment stop halfway. Wat Saket spreads out at the foot of the mount. Highlights include a seated Buddha and murals in the Phra Ubosoth (ordination hall), and a lovely wooden scripture library that dates to the time of Rama I.

MONK'S BOWL VILLAGE

From the library turn right and walk 150m/yds to Thanon Chakkaphatdi Phong. Turn right, then right again at the traffic lights into Thanon Bamrung Muang. After 200m/yds go left into Soi Ban Baat, where the **Monk's Bowl Village ❸** (daily 8am–6pm) is located, 50m/yds on the right.

Although you still see monks carrying metal alms bowls *(baat)* to this day, the bowls are now mainly machine-made, and there are just five families remaining of the original community that moved here from Ayutthaya in the 18th century to make hand-beaten bowls in the new capital. You can hear the alley before

Above from far left: monks contemplate the view on the way up to the Golden Mount; metal alms bowls; Wat Saket.

Below: pointed metal spires of Loha Prasat.

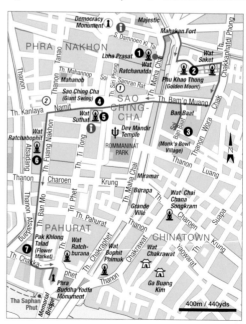

you see it – the noise of hammers clack-clacking on metal as the craftsmen combine each bowl's eight metal pieces, which represent the eight spokes of the Buddhist Dharma Wheel, in turn signifying the Eightfold Path to the end of suffering. The bowls are finished with black lacquer and coloured inscriptions. It takes up to three days to make each one. You can buy them for between B500 and B1,000.

Thanon Bamrung Muang

Leaving the village, go back to Thanon Bamrung Muang and turn left. Cross both the small bridge and the main road (Thanon Maha Chai) and carry on straight ahead. The Old City is full of temples, and this street has typical shops selling accoutrements for Buddhist worship and funeral rites, where monks in orange robes mingle with housewives and businessmen placing orders for ceremonial candles, tiered umbrellas, temple drums, bells and gongs, incense and sparkling lanterns. It is not unusual to see pick-up trucks driving around with 4m (12ft) golden Buddha statues strapped to the back.

GIANT SWING

The square at the end of the road is dominated by the huge teak posts of the **Giant Swing ❹** (Sao Ching Cha). Bangkok's original Giant Swing, erected by King Rama I in 1784, was based on one in Ayutthaya that had been brought to Thailand by Brahman priests in the 16th century. It was used to observe *Triyampawai*, the Brahmin

Below: Giant Swing.

New Year Ceremony, during which four young men in a gondola would swing ever higher, trying to catch purses of gold hanging from poles. The ceremony – a manifestation of a fable in which a serpent swinging between jujube trees tried to topple Shiva and cause the end of the world – was banned in 1931 after several accidents. The swing's original posts were replaced in 2007 with 100-year-old golden teak logs, from which the DNA signature was reportedly taken to be used in the creation of 1 million identical new trees.

If you turn right at the square, on the next corner you will find **Go Pe Shop**, see ⑪①, a typical Chinese shophouse where the owners both live and work.

WAT SUTHAT

To the left of the Giant Swing is **Wat Suthat ❺** (146 Thanon Bamrung Muang; tel: 0 2224 9845; daily 8.30am–9pm; charge), said to have the city's tallest *bot* and also famous for its 8m (26ft) **Phra Sri Sakyamuni Buddha**, the city's largest and oldest cast-bronze Buddha. Its base contains the ashes of King Rama VIII and the walls surrounding it are adorned with spectacular murals depicting incarnations of the Buddha.

King Rama II is said to have helped carve the beautiful doors of the wat, which was begun in 1807, but only completed during the reign of King Rama III (1824–51). The courtyard contains ornamental trees, statues of bronze horses and Chinese stone figures and pagodas.

Meal Break

Come out of Wat Suthat, turn left and go straight across the junction into the small lane ahead. For a meal break, turn right then first lef at the crossroads by the Siam Commercial Bank, and you will come to **Chote Chitr**, 20m/yds on your left, see ①②.

WAT RATCHABOPHIT

Head south where Thanon Kanlaya Namit intersects with Thanon Fuang Nakhon. You will soon come to **Wat Ratchabophit** ❻ (tel: 0 2221 1888; daily 8am–8pm; free), a glittering jewel-box of a temple built in 1870 by Rama V. The *chedi* doors have inlaid mother-of-pearl insignia of the five royal ranks, and the architecture has both Thai and French influences, with outside decoration of benjarong (five-coloured ceramic) tiles and an interior that is akin to a miniature Gothic cathedral. This is typical of its period, which saw many official buildings mix Eastern and European styles. The doors from the street into the temple compound have quaint wooden guardsmen, like toy soldiers, in bas-relief. This square of buildings also houses a school and a cemetery for King Rama V's family.

FLOWER MARKET

Turn right from the wat and cross over the next junction to where the road becomes Thanon Ban Mo, with its bustle of hi-fi market vendors. The shops carry everything from mini DVD players to huge PA stacks, and the roadside is lined with men hunched over trestle tables assembling electronic parts.

Further along on the right is the beginning of the **Flower Market** ❼ (Pak Khlong Talad), which continues into the covered area on the other side of Thanon Chakkaphet, spilling onto streets lined with displays of roses, carnations, sunflowers and myriad orchids. The market occupies a convenient river location to supply funeral wreaths for use in the Old City temples.

Phra Buddha Yodfa Monument

Turn left into Thanon Chakkaphet and after 100m/yds you come to Thanon Tri Phet. On the right, in a garden square, is the **Phra Buddha Yodfa Monument**, a seated statue of King Rama I erected in 1932 to honour Bangkok's 150th anniversary. Either take a taxi from here back to your hotel or walk south past the monument to the Memorial Bridge express boat stop.

Above from far left:
Buddha images at
Wat Suthat; monks
at Wat Ratchabophit.

Night Market
From 7pm to 2am
each night, the
pavements around
the Phra Buddha
Yodfa Monument
come alive with
Saphan Phut Market.
This operates both
from covered stalls
and blankets on the
ground. Among a
wide selection of
goods, the market
is particularly
noted for clothing
and accessories.

Food and Drink

① GO PE SHOP
37 Thanon Siri Phong; tel: 0 2621 0828; daily 7am–8.30pm; $
This is a sweet Chinese corner shop with round marble tables and tasty noodle and rice dishes. Breakfast Set 1 (fried eggs with ground pork) is a favourite, along with fresh Thai coffee from the hills of Chiang Mai.

② CHOTE CHITR
Thanon Praeng Phuton; tel: 0 2221 4082; Mon–Sat 11am–9pm; $
A five-table shophouse opened some 90 years ago by a doctor of traditional medicine. They have served excellent food (and medicines) ever since. Famed for wing-bean salad, *mee krob* and wonderful 'old-fashioned soup'.

5 DUSIT

Leave the fumes of downtown Bangkok far behind, as you take time out in Dusit. Visit a marble temple, paddle around the lake in Dusit Zoo, then stroll among the gardens and palaces of Thailand's most revered king.

DISTANCE 2km (1¼ miles)
TIME A full day
START Wat Benjamabophit
END Royal Paraphernalia Museum
POINTS TO NOTE

As much of this tour includes former palaces and other royal buildings, appropriate dress is required: this means no shorts or sleeveless tops for men or women. If you really are stuck, you can buy or borrow clothes at some sites.

Grand Avenue
King Rama V used the Champs-Elysées in Paris as the model for Thanon Ratchadamnoen Nok, which leads – in three sections – all the way from the Ananta Samakhom Throne Hall to the Grand Palace in Rattanakosin.

The royal enclave at Dusit is so influenced by European architecture, with its wide boulevards and neoclassical domes, that coming here is like entering another country.

WAT BENJAMABOPHIT

Built in 1900 during the reign of Rama V (King Chulalongkorn), **Wat Benjamabophit** ❶ (69 Thanon Rama V; tel: 0 2282 7413; daily 8am–5.30pm; charge) is the last major temple to have been constructed in Bangkok. It has many distinctive elements, including a relaxing manicured garden courtyard with carved stone bridges over a canal. The *viharn* (prayer hall) is designed in cruciform shape, with an exterior of Italian Carrara marble (the wat is also known as the Marble Temple). The stained-glass windows depict praying angels, a radical departure from tradition both in material and subject.

The main Buddha image is a copy of the famed Phra Buddha Jinnarat in the northern town of Phitsanulok, which is said to have wept tears of blood when the town was overrun by Ayutthaya in the 14th century. King Rama V's ashes are buried in its base. The cloisters are lined with Buddha images both from around Thailand and other countries, all with notes on their differing styles.

ROYAL TURF CLUB

For a detour, if you turn right from the temple onto Thanon Sri Ayutthaya and cross Thanon Rama V, you reach the **Royal Turf Club** (183 Thanon Phitsanulok; tel: 0 2628 1810; racing on alternate Sundays; charge). As the centre of horse racing in Thailand, the Turf Club has been organising races and breeding under royal patronage since the reign of King Rama VI (1910–25), as well as managing registrations of horses, trainers and jockeys.

Meetings alternate with those that are held at the Royal Bangkok Sports Club *(see p.58)*. On other days it is a golf club.

KING CHULALONGKORN MONUMENT

Alternatively, turn left from Wat Benjamabophit along Thanon Sri Ayutthaya. Then turn right at the intersection with Thanon Ratchadamnoen Nok, where **Royal Plaza** is home to the equestrian **King Chulalongkorn Monument ❷**. People gather here regularly, but particularly on 23 October, the anniversary of the king's death, to give offerings and wish for luck for themselves in health, business and love. The offerings will often include brandy, whisky or cigars, which the king particularly enjoyed. Royal Plaza also hosts ceremonial occasions such as the Trooping of the Colour on 3 December, when the Royal Guards ceremoniously swear allegiance to the royal family.

ANANTA SAMAKHOM THRONE HALL

Beyond the statue is the **Ananta Samakhom ❸** (Royal Throne Hall; Thanon Uthong Nai; tel: 0 2628 6300–9; daily 10am–4pm; charge), for which construction was started by King Rama V in 1907 as his throne hall. It was finished during the reign of the next king.

Architecturally, this part of Dusit is intrinsically linked to King Rama V, who visited all the major European powers of his time and did much to modernise and internationalise the country *(see feature box, p.48)*. The throne hall is a grand Italianate Renaissance structure containing a domed ceiling with frescoes showing the lives of the king's Chakri-dynasty predecessors painted in 1911–14 by the Italian artist Galileo Chini. The

Above from far left: Wat Benjamabophit.

Muay Thai
A kilometre from Royal Plaza is the Art Deco Ratchadamnoen Stadium (Thanon Ratchadamnoen Nok; tel: 0 2281 4205; charge). This was Bangkok's first Muay Thai (Thai boxing) stadium when it opened in 1945. Fights are held on Monday, Wednesday, Thursday and Sunday.

Below: Ananta Samakhom, the Royal Throne Hall.

Malayan sun bear in Dusit Zoo; Abhisek Dusit Throne Hall; former flag of Siam.

building became Thailand's first parliament after the end of absolute monarchy in 1932, and it still hosts some state occasions.

An exhibition in the hall called the **Arts of the Kingdom** (tel: 0 2283 9411; www.artsofthekingdom.com; Tue–Sun 10am–6pm; charge) has some beautiful reproductions of classical Thai craftsmanship in gold and silver embellished with precious gems, including palanquins, thrones and ceremonial regalia, and a royal table setting, complete with a gold peacock centrepiece.

You can get refreshments on the back lawn at the **Doi Tung**, see ⑪①.

DUSIT ZOO

From the coffee shop take the second gate on the left and turn right onto Thanon Uthong Nai. A short way on the left is the entrance to **Dusit Zoo** ❹ (71 Thanon Rama V; tel: 0 2281 2000; www.zoothailand.org; daily 8am–6pm; charge), which was originally King Rama V's private botanical garden. To skip the zoo visit, turn left on Thanon Uthong Nai, which will bring you to Parliament and Dusit Park.

You could spend a comfortable hour wandering around the zoo. There are trams if you do not want to walk, and maps are dotted around the grounds. In the centre (to the right as you enter) is a lake with an island in the middle and two bridges by which you can cross from one side to the other, or you can potter about the lake on a pedalo (charge).

Royal Projects
Immediately east of Dusit Zoo is Chitralada Palace (tel: 0 2280 4200), the current home of the royal family. It is closed to the public, but with written permission you can visit the Royal Projects, a demonstration of the king's initiative to promote sustainable agriculture, often replacing traditional hill-tribe crops such as opium.

Most of the animals are housed in cages around the edges, and include deer, gibbons, bears, hippos, tigers and lions, but many Thais come here just to hang out away from the heat and fumes of the city.

On the far side of the lake to the right is **Wangwana Kitchen**, see ⑪②, and there are a couple of food courts also in the grounds, offering cheaper fare.

PARLIAMENT

Leave the zoo via the Thanon Ratchawithi gate, close to the tiger house, and turn left, then left again after about 200m/yds into Thanon Uthong Nai. On the right you pass the Thai **Parliament** ❺, which was the scene of several demonstrations between 2006 and 2010 by both supporters and opponents of former Prime Minister Thaksin Shinawatra. The blockades brought government to a standstill, on one occasion forcing MPs to flee over a hedge into Dusit Park.

The statue in the forecourt is of King Rama VII, who was monarch when constitutional government was introduced in 1932. Long-standing plans to relocate Parliament have yet to materialise, but two possible sites are in Nonthaburi and Klong Toey Port.

DUSIT PARK

Beyond Parliament, turn right through the gate immediately after the Elephant Museum to enter **Dusit Park** (Thanon Ratchawithi; tel: 0 2628 6300–9; www.palaces.thai.net; daily 9.30am–4pm;

charge, or included with Grand Palace ticket), home to several museums and former royal buildings.

The **Royal Elephant National Museum**, on the right of the entrance, occupies the former stables of the sacred white elephants, which, when found in the wild, automatically become the property of the king. There are displays of tusks and charms used by elephant handlers *(mahouts)*, photos and articles about elephant capture and training, and a tableau of the ceremony performed during the white elephant presentation. On the left, the **Textile Exhibition Hall** has an array of regional and ethnic woven products.

Abhisek Dusit Throne Hall

Across the lawn is the **Abhisek Dusit Throne Hall** ❻, which was erected in 1903 for King Rama V when he stayed at Vimanmek Mansion *(see below)*. The exterior has a beautiful mix of Victorian 'gingerbread' fretwork and Moorish porticoes. Inside are gold and silverware pieces and examples of niialloware, in which an amalgam of silver, copper and lead is used to add black detailing to carved silver and gold. The technique is commonly associated in Thailand with royalty or people of high office.

Vimanmek Mansion

Walk through the gate on the right of the throne hall, and turn right beyond the pond and stone sculptures. Turn left, cross three bridges and walk past several small museums, including two exhibiting photographs by the current king and another displaying old timepieces. After the third bridge turn left and you will find **Vimanmek Mansion** ❼ 50m/yds on the left. If

White Elephant

The status of the sacred white elephant is connected to the Buddha. His mother is said to have dreamt the night before his birth of a white elephant giving her a lotus flower, the symbol of purity and knowledge. A white elephant on a red background, designed by King Rama IV, was the emblem on the flag of Siam until the current tricolour was adopted in 1917.

Below: Moorish portico at Abhisek Dusit Throne Hall.

Food and Drink 🍴

① DOI TUNG

Ananta Samakhom Throne Hall; no phone; Tue–Sun 10am–8pm; $
Doi Tung is a coffee shop housed in a handsome white pavilion, in which cookies, Thai coffee from Chiang Mai, and mushroom, chicken and tuna pies are sold. Beware: the pastry is sweet.

② WANGWANA KITCHEN

Dusit Zoo; tel: 0 2282 1491; daily 11.30am–11.30pm; $–$$
This lakeside *sala* restaurant with open walls is a good spot to watch the boating, while eating such things as steamed seafood coconut curry or jungle curry with sun-dried pork.

Wat Ratchathiwat
Consider making
a detour to
Wat Ratchathiwat
(658 Samsen 9; tel:
0 2243 2125; daily
5am–9pm), which
is interesting for its
Western-style murals
by Carlo Rigoli, who
also worked on the
Ananta Samakhom
Throne Hall. The
chedi here has four
9th-century Buddha
images from Java.
King Rama IV stayed
at the wat for part of
the time he lived as a
monk, from 1824–51.

you turn right here by the ATM machines you come to **Wang Ying**, see ③.

Entry to the mansion is only allowed as part of a tour, conducted at half-hourly intervals, lasting around 45 minutes, and visiting 30 of the 81 rooms. Vimanmek, or 'Cloud Mansion' was originally built in 1868 on the island of Koh Si Chang, on the eastern seaboard, but King Rama V, influenced by seeing royal residences with spacious gardens on the outskirts of European capitals, moved it to Bangkok in 1901.

The mansion is touted as the largest golden teak building in the world, and incorporates Thai, Italian and Victorian styles. The collection inside is equally eclectic, being a mishmash of local artefacts and objects that caught the eye of the king on his travels to the West, such

as the brass bathtub, which may have been the first of its kind in Siam. Vimanmek was certainly the first Thai building with indoor sanitation, and also with electricity.

The king sent many of his children abroad to study, and one of the many photos on display shows him in England surrounded by a dozen of his sons: in all he had 77 children, born of 40 concubines. Among the glassware, silver and ceramics are small containers covered with precious stones, gold and ivory. These were used for storing betel leaves and areca nuts, which at the time were chewed even by royalty as a stimulant, staining the teeth red.

Royal Paraphernalia Museum
Leave Vimanmek from the entrance you came in and walk straight ahead for 100m/yds. On the left is another display hall and, running around it, the wonderfully named **Royal Paraphernalia Museum**, which has exhibits such as antique palanquins, ceremonial gongs and Victorian hansom cabs that were made to order in London.

The gate ahead leads to Thanon Ratchawithi, where you can catch a taxi back to your hotel.

King Chulalongkorn

King Chulalongkorn (Rama V) is so revered in Thailand that his photograph is still widely displayed in homes and places of work. He ascended the throne aged 15 in 1868, under the initial guidance of a regent, and is often credited with warding off the attentions of Britain and France, through clever diplomacy: Siam was the only Southeast Asian nation not to be colonised. After his travels to Europe and to Asian countries such as Singapore that had been colonised, Chulalongkorn returned with many ideas that helped modernise Siam. Regarding education, he said: 'All of our subjects, from our royal children down to the lowest commoners, will have the same opportunity to study.' He also abolished slavery in 1905, centralised government, introduced mapping and the postal service, and remodelled the judiciary, medical and banking systems.

Food and Drink 🍴
③ **WANG YING**
Dusit Park; no phone; daily
10am–3pm; $
A simple café staffed by students of the Women's College in the Grand Palace. Dishes include crabmeat fried rice with clear soup, and Chinese cabbage with salty fish.

CHINATOWN

Chinatown has been hugely influential in Bangkok life since the beginning of the city. It is the centre of the gold trade, and has a 200-year-old market, Taoist temples, and a 5-ton solid-gold Buddha at Wat Traimit.

The beginnings of a real Chinatown came when King Taksin encouraged Teochew labourers and merchants to relocate from southern China in 1767, when he chose Thonburi, on the opposite side of the river, as his new capital. King Rama I later moved the immigrants downstream when he claimed land to build the Grand Palace in 1872. Chinatown's boundaries now stretch along the Chao Phraya, loosely from River City shopping complex to the edge of Pahurat Market.

WAT TRAIMIT

Wat Traimit ❶ (661 Thanon Charoen Krung; tel: 0 2225 9775; daily

DISTANCE 2.75km (1¾ miles)
TIME A full day
START Wat Traimit
END Pahurat Market
POINTS TO NOTE
You can get to Wat Traimit either by taxi or by metro to Hualamphong Station and then a taxi.

8am–5pm; charge) contains the world's largest solid-gold Buddha, and is consequently known also as the Temple of the Golden Buddha. On the left of the temple as you enter the grounds is a huge 600 million baht marble *mondop* (pavilion) built in 2009

Above from far left:
Vimanmek Mansion; detail of a Chinese dragon.

First Chinese
Early Chinese traders had been coming through Bangkok since the Ayutthaya period, bringing luxury goods such as porcelain, which they exchanged mainly for rice.

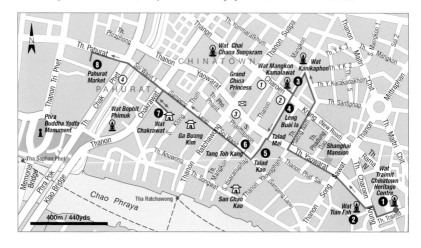

Growth of Chinatown
Once they had settled in Bangkok, many Chinese grew wealthy investing in rice mills, sawmills and *godowns* (warehouses). As their merchant influence grew, so did their access to the corridors of power through relationships with royalty and, later, politicians, who controlled the avenues to smooth trade. Today, many politicians, including former prime minister Thaksin Shinawatra, are Chinese-Thai.

Below: signs of Chinatown.

to house the 5.5-ton, 3m (10ft) Sukhothai-era statue, which is believed to date from the reign of King Ramkhamhaeng the Great (*c.*1279–98). The statue was probably first moved from Sukhothai to Ayutthaya, but by the time it reached Bangkok it had been covered in stucco, presumably to disguise its worth from Burmese invaders. Its true nature was only revealed in 1955, when an accident while moving it caused the surface to crack off.

The *mondop* is also the location of the **Yaowarat Chinatown Heritage Centre** (daily 8am–4.30pm; charge), opened in 2008. The museum layout is preceded by a 3-D hologram show of a grandfather and grandson discussing the past, which is only interesting for the comically 'proper' English translation. The museum tells the story of Chinatown's beginnings through old photos, prints of period paintings and tableaux of such things as the interior of a junk and shops from old Sampeng Lane. Exhibits are well annotated, and it makes an interesting sideshow when visiting the Golden Buddha.

Stalls close by sell items ranging from 'Amazing Thailand' T-shirts to little crystal tuk tuks, leaving the impression that the temple is very much a commercial enterprise.

THANON YAOWARAT

Leaving the temple, turn right on Thanon Traimit and walk to the Odeon Circle with its Chinatown ceremonial arch. Turn right, passing the

'Golden Shine Foundation' with its Happy Buddha in the doorway, and the offices of the Chinese Clans Relations Cultural Centre, and cross Thanon Charoen Krung. Head northwest along Thanon Yaowarat.

Wat Tian Fah

On the left is **Wat Tian Fah** ❷ (7am–5pm) and its adjacent hospital. Temples were traditional places of healing, where monks used many of the herbal treatments now popular in spas. Wat Tian Fah has a 2.5m (8ft) golden statue of Guan Yin, Goddess of Mercy, who people pray to for recovery from illness.

Commercial Hub

By the next corner you start to smell the aromas of Five Spice, that mix of star anise, cloves, cinnamon, fennel and Szechuan peppercorns so redolent of Chinese cooking. Shop signs are now in Chinese as well as Thai; restaurants advertise specialities like bird's nest soup; windows proudly display whole sharks' fins (the fins are sliced off and the sharks thrown back live to sink to the bottom and die).

Look upwards at the buildings opposite for examples of 1930s Thai Art Deco. On the right, after crossing Thanon Song Sawat, look out for the Tops supermarket. Above it sits the beautiful 1930s retro **Shanghai Mansion**, one of Bangkok's new breed of boutique hotels *(see p.111)*.

Thanon Yaowarat is known as Thailand's 'Gold Street', and across the road you see the first of the large gold shops for which the area is as famous

as for its food. Locals use the precious metal as emergency savings, buying and selling often to meet cash-flow demands. Dealers display the day's price, like bank exchange rates, in baat measures (1 baat = 15.2 grammes).

Cross Thanon Phadung Dao (where two famous seafood stalls, **Rut & Lek** and **T & K**, open for dinner at 6pm daily), and then turn right at Thanon Plaeng Nam. Immediately on the left is a small store that sells masks and costumes for use in Chinese Opera and the Lion Dances that rattle and drum through the streets at Chinese New Year.

THANON PHLAPPHLACHAI

At the top of the street, cross Thanon Charoen Krung into Thanon Phlapphlachai and follow the road as it bends left. This street serves the many temples in the area with red-and-gold displays of paper temple banners and 3m (10ft) tall incense sticks. The traders use paper with designs resembling banknotes to fold into various items that will be burnt as funeral offerings, a practice called *kong tek*. These are for the comfort of the deceased in their next life and include models of cars, houses and mobile phones. They also sell altars and spirit houses for use in ancestor worship.

TROK ITSARANUPHAP

At the end of the bend turn left into Thanon Yommaratkhum and left again, immediately, into Trok Itsaranuphap.

This has more the feel of the original Chinatown, of hectic alleys and shops selling eclectic products. Old ladies beneath umbrellas are flanked by tangles of mysterious root vegetables and fresh fish in bamboo trays that they gut before your eyes and dispense wrapped in banana-leaf packets. Delicious deep-fried pork lies stacked in rounds like broken bike tyres. Thirty metres/yds on the right, Khun Lakyat cooks fantastic soup in a deep vat over charcoal. Bright-red chillies and whole fish lie on the surface, each topped with a small mound of grated ginger. She spoons it

Vegetarian Festival

Each year for nine days at the start of the ninth lunar month (usually early October) vegetarian festivals are held all over the country. During this Chinese Taoist event participants wear white and abstain from meat, alcohol and sex. Some also avoid vegetables that overstimulate the senses, such as onion, celery and garlic.

The festival in Bangkok centres around and between Thanon Yaowarat and Thanon Charoen Krung, which become a sea of yellow flags, signifying participating restaurants and food stalls. Many Thai and Chinese restaurants in other parts of the capital also offer special vegetarian menus.

Dragon parades, cooking demonstrations and spectacular Chinese opera are all crowd-pleasers. And you may also see acts of self-mutilation in which devotees under trance pierce their flesh with knives and skewers, although these acts are more famous and more common at the festival on Phuket.

With the Bangkok events alone generating some B2 billion (around US $60 million), the festival is big business. High demand, and a bit of opportunism, forces up the price of vegetables so much during the festival that sometimes the government subsidises 'Fresh Vegetable Fairs' to sell low-cost greens to the public.

Daughters' Duty
From the 18th century, several Chinese daughters became royal consorts. King Taksin was Chinese, and many Chakri kings, including Rama IX, have Chinese forebears.

into plastic bags knotted with elastic bands for people to take home at B60 a portion. Beyond the food stalls there are clothes, crockery, trinkets, and more funerary items.

Wat Mangkon Kamalawat

Take a small detour by turning right at Thanon Charoen Krung to reach **Wat Mangkon Kamalawat ❸** (tel: 0 2222 3975; daily 6am–5pm; free), which is Chinatown's biggest temple. Built in 1871, it is a place of worship for Mahayana Buddhists whose beliefs differ from those of the Thai Theravadist tradition. The building – originally named Wat Leng Noi Yee (Dragon Flower Temple) until changed by King Rama V – has Chinese and Tibetan inscriptions at the entrance, introducing a hallway display of fearsome Thao Chatulokaban (the four guardians of the world) in ornate warrior costumes. Along with Buddha images, there are statues inside of saintly figures, including one of the man who financed the temple building. Wat Mangkon Kamalawat is the

centre point for the Vegetarian Festival each October *(see feature box, p.51)*.

Lunch Stops

Leaving the temple, if you turn right along Thanon Charoen Krung, after 100m/yds you will spy the bustling **Hua Seng Hong Yaowaraj**, see ⓘ① on the left, which is a good place to eat.

To continue the tour turn left from the temple and cross the road into the continuation of Trok Itsaranuphap, which from here also adopts the name Charoen Krung Soi 16. Many streets in Bangkok have several names – old and new official names and sometimes even a third based on local usage associated with an area landmark. A short way into the *soi* is **Hong Kong Noodle**, see ⓘ②, an alternative lunch stop.

Leng Buai Ia

Another 30m/yds on the left brings you to the small courtyard of **Leng Buai Ia ❹**, which has a plaque inside dated 1685, making it the oldest Chinese shrine in Bangkok. The roof has glazed patterned tiles and a pair of stucco dragons, with dragon motifs also on the doorposts and inner pillars. The wooden interior is partly open to the elements and has a temple bell to the right of the altar that dates to the late 19th-century Qing dynasty.

Continuing down Itsaranuphap, the trays of fleshy black *ping talay* (sea cucumber), fresh meats, pastries and fruit mark an area called **Talad Mai** (New Market). Coming to Thanon Yaowarat, you could turn left and

Food and Drink

① HUA SENG HONG YAOWARAJ
438 Charoen Krung Soi 14; tel: 0 2627 5030; $–$$
A busy air-conditioned café that sells all-day dim sum from an outside counter and all manner of congee, hot and sour soup, barbecued pork, fish maw and braised goose-web dishes inside.

② HONG KONG NOODLE
136/4 Trok Itsaranuphap; tel: 0 2623 1992; $
You will probably have to wait for a seat at this jammed alley shophouse, where cooks in constant motion ladle duck and pork onto noodles. Grab a custard tart at Hong Kong Dim Sum (no relation) next door for dessert.

finish the walk back at the Odeon Circle, from where you can take a taxi home, or cross the street to the continuation of Itsaranuphap (by now called Yaowarat Soi 11). Here your nostrils are assailed by the tangy salt smells of preserved shrimp and squid, heralding the entrance on the left of **Talad Kao ❺** (Old Market), which has been in business for 200 years.

SAMPENG LANE

Moving past the market, the alley crossing 150m/yds ahead is **Sampeng Lane** (also called Soi Wanit 1), Chinatown's original thoroughfare in the late 18th century. The early Chinese immigrants toiled as labourers, rickshaw runners and dock workers at a time when the river was filled with wooden shops and houses floating on bamboo platforms. They ran two and three lines deep amid a constant clutter of trading vessels and cross-river traffic. Sampeng Lane was the trading ground for landlubbers, and though many of the wares will be new, many haven't changed since that time, and neither has the sense of chaos. Hence the lane is best explored with a sense of adventurous curiosity, breaking off from the itinerary as the mood takes you.

Dodging scooters laden with crates, you will pass stalls with dresses, bags, footwear, toys, party decorations, Thai flags, Chinese dice, sparkling acrylic bracelets and semi-precious stones for making your own jewellery. Most of it is available wholesale as well as retail.

Tang Toh Kang

At the junction of Soi Mangkon (or Sanjao Mai), on the right is the handsome facade of **Tang Toh Kang ❻**, the oldest goldsmith in Bangkok. Originally opened around 1880 further down Soi Mangkon, the business moved to these premises 90 years ago. It has a museum upstairs with gold items and examples of early crafting tools. On the opposite corner is a building from a similar period, once a gold shop, now a bank.

If you are tired after the next section of Sampeng Lane, you could turn left along Thanon Ratchawong and catch an express boat from Tha Ratchawong. Alternatively, you might be hungry now; if you turn right, and then right again at Thanon Yaowarat, you will come to **Shangrila Yaowarat**, see ⓫③ *(p.54)*.

Above from far left: Chinese teashop; food for sale at Talad Kao market.

Dens of Iniquity
By the turn of the 20th century, Sampeng Lane was notorious for its opium dens, gambling parlours and 'green-light' houses, the equivalent of Western red-light districts.

Below: main entrance to Wat Chakrawat.

Above from left:
ceremonial gate
in Chinatown;
floral offerings at
Erawan Shrine.

WAT CHAKRAWAT

Moving on along Sampeng, the lane is now covered overhead and lined with fabric merchants. At the junction with Thanon Chakrawat, turn left and walk 100m/yds to the large stone gates beside the old Chinese herbalist and turn into **Wat Chakrawat** ❼ (7.30am–5pm). After 70m/yds go through the ornate gate on your left and turn right, where there is a grotto seemingly modelled on a cave temple, with small alcoves for offerings, a mural and several statues. One of the latter is of a fat man; local legend says he was a very handsome monk who was frequently pestered by women while deep in meditation. He responded by eating until he was so fat the women lost interest. The statue was built to honour his religious devotion.

Temple Resident

Returning towards the gate, climb the small wall overlooking the tiny pond between two *prang* (spires), and see if you can spot the croc. People often take animals to wats to be cared for *(see p.80)*, and this one has been the re-cipient of several crocodiles over the years. The original – said to be a half-blind specimen called 'One-Eyed Guy' that terrorised the canals – is displayed in a glass case above the water.

BACK ON SAMPENG

Retrace your steps, turn left into Sampeng Lane and stroll past the stalls of beads, brocade, bangles and frills. The lane climbs a small humpbacked

bridge over Khlong Ong Ang. If you turn left into the alley immediately after it you will find **Punjab Sweets and Restaurant**, see ⑪④, after 150m/yds. The aromas are distinctly different here at the edge of Pahurat, Bangkok's Little India.

PAHURAT MARKET

At the end of Sampeng Lane, cross the road into Thanon Pahurat; 50m/yds on the left is **Kwan**, a small shop selling Thai classical and folk dance costumes and masks. At 100m/yds duck into **Pahurat Market** ❽ (9am–6pm) and root around in a two-floor emporium of all things Indian.

Catch a taxi home or go past the market and turn left at Thanon Tri Phet. After 15 minutes you will come to Memorial Bridge express boat pier.

Culinary Mix
The Chinese have had a major influence on Thai food, particularly with the introduction of noodles, which come in multiple forms and are the country's single most popular lunch time meal.

Food and Drink 🍴

③ SHANGRILA YAOWARAT
306 Thanon Yaowarat;
tel: 0 2224 5933; $$
The casual dim sum lunches here make way for the tablecloths and napkins at dinner. The menu then includes drunken chicken with jelly-fish, smoked pigeon, and seafood from tanks on the ground floor.

④ PUNJAB SWEETS AND RESTAURANT
436/5 Thanon Chak Phet;
tel: 0 2623 7606; $
This small vegetarian café (also with dairy-free options) features South Indian curries, great-value *thalis* (a bit of everything), *dosas* (rice-flour pancakes) and Punjabi sweets wrapped in edible silver foil.

PATHUMWAN

On this tour you can drink snake's blood in Lumphini Park, dive with sharks at Siam Ocean World or blow all your money in the malls around Siam Square. It is not a day trip for the faint-hearted, although you will end in the serenity of the Jim Thompson House Museum.

The commercial heart of downtown Bangkok, Pathumwan is a sprawl of shopping malls. While it is mainly a consumer's paradise, there are still plenty of sights more reminiscent of an older and more traditional Bangkok.

LUMPHINI PARK

Bangkok has few green spaces, and even the biggest, **Lumphini Park ❶**, covering 58ha (142 acres), is relatively small. Enter by the southeastern gate, unmistakable for its statue of Rama VI in the entrance square. This king owned the land when it was known as Saladaeng Field, until he donated it to the nation as a public park and fairground in 1925. He brought plants from around Thailand and renamed it Lumphini after the Buddha's birthplace in Nepal. The Chinese pagoda-like clock tower was built the same year. Nearby is the Lumphini Park Public Library, the first of its kind in Thailand.

Outdoor Retreat

Until 9am the park is busy with weightlifters, joggers and people practising martial arts on the grass before the sun gets too hot. If you are lucky you may come across a stall selling shots of snake's blood, believed to be

DISTANCE 4.5km (2¾ miles)
TIME A full day
START Lumphini Park
END Ban Krua
POINTS TO NOTE

Start the tour by taxi to the Lumphini Park gate on the corner of Thanon Rama IV and Thanon Ratchadamri, or ride a Skytrain to Sala Daeng or the metro to Silom and cross Thanon Rama IV. This is a long tour, but it is all close to public transport, so you can easily break off at any time.

Kites and Concerts
Lumphini Park is flecked with kite-fliers from February to April, and in the cool season, from December to March, the park hosts open-air classical concerts every Sunday.

Below: enjoying the view and tranquillity of Lumphini Park.

Snakes Alive
Some 400m/yds from the entrance of Lumphini Park is the Snake Farm (1871 Thanon Rama IV; tel: 0 2252 0161; www.redcross.or.th; charge), with demonstrations of venom milking at 11am.

a general cure-all and aphrodisiac. You may also see pick-up games of *takraw*, a traditional sport similar to tennis, but played with the feet. Monitor lizards swim and roam around the edges of the artificial lake, where you can potter about in hired boats.

ERAWAN SHRINE

Come out of the park at any gate and hail a taxi to the **Erawan Shrine ❷**. The three-headed elephant Erawan, which features in Hindu mythology, makes many appearances in Thai life, but the Erawan Shrine is actually dedicated to Brahma, the four-headed Hindu God of Creation. It was erected in 1956 after an astrologer advised it would ward off the bad luck that was plaguing construction of the Erawan Hotel (now the Grand Hyatt Erawan), after which it was named. As the misfortune subsequently ceased, people believe the shrine has great powers, and it has become one of Bangkok's most visited.

Revered Place of Worship
Throughout the day people walking by or travelling in cars press their palms together to *wai (see p.101)* the shrine as they pass, and supplicants line up amid clouds of incense to buy garlands, joss sticks and other gifts as offerings in return for good fortune. Those whose wishes are granted might give thanks by paying the on-site dance troupe to perform.

The site is so revered that when a mentally disturbed man smashed the shrine with a hammer in 2006, he was beaten to death by an angry mob. Four photographs of the shrine were displayed so that people could continue to worship until a new one was erected two months later: 1,000 people attended the unveiling. Underlining the huge influence of supernatural belief in Thailand, an opposition leader accused supporters of then Prime Minister Thaksin Shinawatra of being responsible for the destruction, saying they wanted to maintain power over the country through black magic.

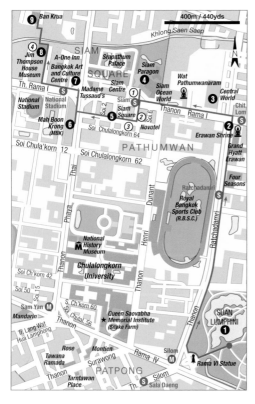

SHOPPING STREET

From the shrine turn right onto Thanon Ploenchit and climb the stairs to Chit Lom Skytrain Station in order to access the overhead skywalk that runs beneath the tracks for several hundred metres in each direction. As this stretch contains many of the city's premier malls, it has been optimistically marketed as the city's Shopping Street, the answer to Singapore's Orchard Road. However, Bangkok's pavements are cluttered, crowded and uneven, so despite being featureless in itself, the skywalk actually does make movement between shops easier.

Central World

Turn left at the top of the stairs and after passing over the crossroads, turn right into **Central World** ❸ (999/9 Thanon Rama I; tel: 0 2264 5555; www.centralworld.co.th), Bangkok's biggest shopping mall at 800,000 sq m (957,000 sq yds). It is owned by Central Group, a major Thai success story: having started as a humble Chinatown magazine shop in 1927, it now has over 200 stores throughout the country, with a turnover in excess of US $1.5 billion. In 1956 it was the first shop in the country to have fixed pricing. The mall is packed with high-street brands – fashion, sports, electronics, toys, cosmetics and restaurants.

Siam Paragon

Leave Central World via the skywalk and turn right. After 400m/yds the path dog-legs to the left, ending at the Siam Skytrain Station concourse. Turn right over the walkway into **Siam Paragon** ❹ (Thanon Rama I; tel: 0 2658 3000; www.siamparagon.co.th), another mega mall with cinemas, concert space and 250 stores. Fashion takes up 30 percent of Bangkok's retail area, so it is no surprise that names like Cartier, Chanel and Jimmy Choo feature strongly, along with hip Thai labels such as Greyhound. Level four has Kinokunya, which is probably the city's best bookstore, while on level two you can walk among Ferraris and Lamborghinis displayed like dresses in shop windows.

On the ground level is a classy supermarket, a good wine shop and many restaurants, including **Savoury**, see 🍴① *(p.58)*, as well as a good and cheap food court, where you buy coupons to exchange for dishes of curry, noodles and salads, plus Western fare such as burgers, pasta and pizzas.

Siam Ocean World

In the Siam Paragon basement is **Siam Ocean World** (tel: 0 2687 2000; www.siamoceanwold.co.th; charge), an underwater arena with 400 aquatic species displayed in seven zones. Highlights include giant spider crabs, cuddly water rats, otters that frolic like kittens, and candiru, Amazonian blood-sucking fish that can swim into human orifices and drink their fill. Among local species on show is the archer fish, which spits spumes of water to bring down insects hovering above the surface. Farmers traditionally used them to keep pests from rice paddies.

Above from far left: shop 'til you drop at Siam Paragon; feeding time at Siam Ocean World.

Beer Garden
In the cool season, the square outside Central World becomes a beer garden with rock bands and large-screen TVs. This is also the location for Bangkok's New Year Countdown, similar to the one held in London's Trafalgar Square.

Royal Relics
The handsome Wat Pathumwanaram, next to Central World, contains the ashes of the king's mother and his father, Prince Mahidol, who was the 69th child of King Rama V.

Most spectacular is the transparent underwater tunnel allowing close-ups of all 300 sharks' teeth and bizarre face-to-face meetings with stingrays. There are regular animal-feeding displays, glass-bottomed-boat trips and diving with the sharks. A fun 4-D ecological movie (the fourth D is sensory) has the audience – both children and adults – screaming with delight.

SIAM SQUARE

From Siam Paragon, go back to the Skytrain station concourse, cross to the other side and walk down the steps to the street. Carry straight on and turn into the first road on the left, Siam Square Soi 5. At the end, on the left, is the busy Isaan restaurant **Somtam Siam Square Soi 5**, see ②.

Turn right into **Siam Square** ❺, a grid of *sois* that crosses land owned by Thailand's most prestigious educational institution, Chulalongkorn University, which is located on the southern edge of the square. Unsurprisingly, the square is packed with students and has a strong youth culture, including its own radio station with blaring street speakers that drown out the noise of the traffic. For many years it has been a hotbed of tyro fashion designers who sell imaginative clothes in boutique shops with eccentric names like 'It's Happened to Be a Closet'. Recent rent hikes by the university, however, may be signalling the gradual demise of this creative zone.

Walk on – turning left at Soi 9 if you want to stop off to eat at student-friendly **Inter**, see ①③ – and continue past the Hard Rock Café to the end of the road, where **Bonanza Mall** sells T-shirts, dresses and funky pumps from as little as B150. Sizes will be Thai (ie small), so will probably suit early teens rather than standard-size adults.

Food and Drink

① SAVOURY

Ground Floor, Siam Paragon, Thanon Rama I; tel: 0 2129 4353; $$
A stylish café with bright cushions and marble tables. Lemongrass chicken with mixed fruits in a delicious *somtam* dressing is typical of the inventive touches here. Good cakes and a range of teas are also served.

② SOMTAM SIAM SQUARE SOI 5

392/2 Siam Square Soi 5; tel: 0 2251 4880; $
This modern Isaan restaurant features an island kitchen that produces treats such as spicy salads, sticky rice and northeastern sausage. So popular there are cushions outside for people waiting.

③ INTER

432/1–2 Siam Square Soi 9; tel: 0 2251 4689; $
Popular student hang-out Inter offers unusual dishes like spicy steamed shrimp in lemonade alongside more usual fare such as crispy fried catfish salad and grilled mussels.

Sport of Kings

Five hundred metres/yds from Siam Square is the Royal Bangkok Sports Club (1 Thanon Henri Dunant; tel: 0 2255 1420; www.rbsc.org), an elite members' hang-out that throws open its doors to the public every other Saturday for horse-race meetings. King Rama V donated the land specifically for this purpose in 1902, and some claim the royal charter is the chief reason why the sport retains its gambling licence despite some government opposition. Gambling is generally illegal in Thailand (along with racing, only Muay Thai boxing and the National Lottery are licensed), so only on-course betting is allowed; don't place bets with the illegal bookies ouside. You can hire binoculars for a better view.

MAH BOON KRONG

Beyond the mall turn left onto Thanon Phaya Thai. After 50m/yds climb the stairs over the footbridge to **Mah Boon Krong ❻** (MBK; 444 Thanon Phaya Thai; tel: 0 2620 9000; www.mbk center.com). This huge old-school Thai mall retains a marketplace ambience, with stalls scattered around the floor-space between shops selling a vast array of goods, including cosmetics, cameras, phones, clothes and jewellery. Art-lovers head for the ground floor, where teams of painters copy masters from Titian to Klimt for a few thousand baht apiece. The fourth floor has software and DVD stores; there is a food court on five; and the top level is dominated by a bowling alley, cinema and karaoke booths. MBK's market approach also means you can bargain at many stalls. It is always worth a try.

BANGKOK ART AND CULTURE CENTRE

Leave MBK via the Tokyu department store exit to the National Stadium Skytrain Station bridge on the second floor. Walk straight ahead and cross the footbridge into the 11-storey **Bangkok Art and Culture Centre ❼** (939 Thanon Rama I; tel: 0 2214 6630–8; www.bacc.or.th). This space stages some of Bangkok's best art and multimedia shows, featuring both local and international artists and also has occasional live performances. Its retail outlets include independent galleries and organisations like the Thai Film Foundation and Bangkok Opera.

Above from far left:
youthful Siam Square;
Skytrain station.

Madame Tussaud's
Madame Tussaud's
(FI6 Siam Discovery
Centre; tel: 0 2658
0060; www.madame
tussauds.com/
bangkok; charge)
opened in 2010 with
waxwork models of
local celebrities and
international stars
such as Madonna,
Michael Jackson and
Angelina Jolie.

Left: escalator
at MBK.

Enigmatic End
The mystery of Thompson's wartime profession is thought by some to be linked to his abrupt disappearance. In 1967, while on holiday in Malaysia's Cameron Highlands, he failed to return from a walk; his disappearance is an unsolved case.

JIM THOMPSON HOUSE MUSEUM

From the gallery turn right onto Thanon Rama I. On the opposite side of the road is the **National Stadium**, venue for various sports, including football and athletics. After 200m/yds turn right into Soi Kasemsan 2 and walk to the end to find the **Jim Thompson House Museum** ❼ (6 Soi Kasem San 2; tel: 0 2216 7368; www.jimthompson house.com; charge). Jim Thompson was an American operative for the OSS, forerunner of the CIA, during World War II. In the latter stages of the war he served as an OSS station chief in Bangkok, and afterwards remained in Thailand. It was then that he spied the profitable potential of Thai silk; at the time the material was undervalued even in Thailand itself. Clever marketing saw his fabrics used extensively in the 1956 film *The King & I*, starring Yul Brynner. The movie − banned in Thailand for disrespectful portrayal of the monarchy − was a major influence in securing an international market for Thai silk.

The former architect also appreciated traditional Thai houses and he transported several single rooms from upcountry to reconstruct them in Bangkok. Traditional Thai houses are built without nails, which means that they can easily be taken down and relocated. On getting married, for instance, a groom would dismantle his room and attach it to his bride's family home, adding to the cluster of buildings in which extended families traditionally lived. Thompson's house is a typical cluster arrangement, now rarely seen in Thailand. The collection of antiques inside is particularly strong on religious art and porcelain. Regular guided tours of the house take around 30 minutes.

Also in the grounds are top-quality silk and souvenir shops, and the minimalist **Jim Thompson Bar & Restaurant**, see ⑪④.

BAN KRUA

Thompson constructed his house opposite the canalside Muslim village of **Ban Krua** ❽. Its inhabitants were specialist silk weavers whose ancestors moved here from Cambodia in the 19th century. There are just two workshops still active, which you can visit by turning left from the Jim Thompson House Museum, then left again along the canal. After 150m/yds cross the bridge and walk on to a small lane on the right. Just along here, a handful of women at looms keep alive a traditional craft that captivated the world. In the second shop you may be lucky enough to catch owner Niphon Manuthas, who as a young boy knew Jim Thompson himself.

Food and Drink 🍴
④ JIM THOMPSON BAR & RESTAURANT
6 Soi Kasem San 2; tel: 0 2216 7368; $$
A contemporary setting of brushed concrete and stone is softened by plenty of silk cushions. In addition to a general Thai menu, there are regional choices and a Western selection offering pasta, burgers and sandwiches. Indoor and outdoor seating.

SILOM

After dark, Bangkok's business district bursts with a different kind of life. The bubble of night markets, Thai boxing, elegant puppet theatre and the notorious go-go bars of Patpong are best seen after sunset cocktails with stupendous river views at The Dome.

As the only official nightlife zone in the city centre, the top end of Thanon Silom offers guaranteed late-night drinking. With so many bars packed closely together, there is a friendly, festival-like bustle that makes it one of the most enjoyable areas of the city.

THE DOME

Start the tour with a breathtaking Bangkok panorama: take the elevator to **The Dome** ❶ (63/F, State Tower, 1055/111 Thanon Silom; tel: 0 2624 9555; www.thedomebkk.com; daily 6pm–1am), a complex of restaurants and bars that sits atop the city's second-highest skyscraper, with Bangkok's highest balcony.

Sirocco

The original and most famous restaurant here is the five-star **Sirocco** *(see*

DISTANCE 2km (1¼ miles)
TIME A half day
START The Dome
END Thanon Silom
POINTS TO NOTE

Best started just before sunset, and on Tue, Fri or Sat for Thai boxing. Smart-casual dress code at The Dome, so no shorts or sandals for men.

Above from far left: antiques inside the Jim Thompson House Museum; moment of impact in a Muay Thai event.

Below: admire the view from the Sirocco restaurant's terrace at The Dome.

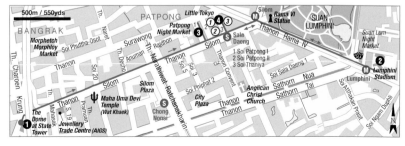

p.120). It is 200m (656ft) above ground and open to the wind, so the crow's-nest view of downtown lights could blow you away. On one side there is spotlit garden landscaping and a sweeping staircase with a jazz band at the top, on the other a sheer drop to the street below. The Greco-Roman setting – all Doric columns topped by a gold dome – may seem incongruous, but Euro-Asian architecture has a pedigree stretching back over a century and is, in fact, very Bangkok. If you want to dine here it is best to book ahead. However, many people come just to soak up the panorama with a couple of cocktails at the **Sky Bar**. Not cheap, but not to be missed.

THAI BOXING

Next grab a taxi on the opposite side of the road to **Lumphini Stadium** ❷ (Thanon Rama IV; tel: 0 2252 8765; matches on Tue 6.15–11pm, Fri–Sat 5–8pm and 8.30pm–midnight; charge), which will cost around B60. This is Thailand's most famous Muay Thai venue, featuring some of the country's best fighters. The sport, although brutal – arms, elbows, knees and feet are all used – is highly ritualised, with the contestants initially performing a *wai kru* dance of respect for their trainers. A traditional Thai *pipat* band sits ringside accompanying the action with a wailing of pipes and reeds. The crowd becomes increasingly animated as the punches rain – you can hear the roars from outside – and the betting action is a whirlwind of arms signal-

ling odds and wagers across the arena. Thai kickboxing is one of two sports (the other is horse racing) that are exempt from laws prohibiting gambling in Thailand. Many of the boxers will have started their careers at seven years old at village temple fairs around the country, earning around B50 for their first fights. If they're good, within a few years they will be their family's main breadwinner. You can get a feel of the atmosphere in the stadium forecourt, where shops sell boxing paraphernalia, or go inside to watch a few bouts.

PATPONG

Now take a taxi (B40) to **Patpong** ❸, which became one of Bangkok's first Western-oriented red-light areas when it opened in the 1960s to cater to US GIs on R&R from the Vietnam War. Depending on your tolerance levels, there is a surprisingly unsleazy ambience here, and despite the ongoing sex trade, its two *sois* – Patpong I and II – have become prime tourist attractions, enhanced by a busy night market that runs along Soi I.

Nevertheless, you will still be hassled by touts flashing menu cards with a list of notorious ping-pong acrobatics, and surprisingly these – along with ground floor go-go bars with girls pole dancing in bikinis – are also visited by some women tourists, who drop in for a peek at Bangkok's seamier side. In fact, this type of invitation card has a long history. In 1923 the writer Somerset Maugham

Love In

Silom is in an area called Bangrak, which means 'Village of Love'. Consequently, every St Valentine's Day the district office is besieged by hundreds of couples wanting to be married in a lucky place on an auspicious day.

recorded a man giving him a card offering the services of 'Miss Pretty Girl', who would 'put him in dreamland with perfumed soap'.

Patpong Night Market

The night market here sells all manner of fake goods, including T-shirts, jeans, CDs, handbags and the notorious Rolex watches. Coming from Thanon Silom, walk up the left-hand side of the stalls (after 100m/yds, look out for Radio City, a small bar that features Elvis Presley impersonators on Thursday and Friday nights), do a U-turn at the top and come back down either the middle or the other side. The opening prices will start high, but be brave with your responses and you will be surprised by how easily – and how far – they come down.

There is a lively atmosphere here, with all walks of life – pimps, punters, ladyboys, and shoppers from every country imaginable – and the tables outside bars are perfect for watching them all walk by. While Soi II has no market it does have the French bistro Le Bouchon, see ⑴①.

SILOM NIGHTLIFE

You can end the tour at Patpong, but if you fancy a nightcap and Patpong doesn't do it for you, head back to Thanon Silom and turn left. The main road here contains the overspill of Patpong, with lots more stalls selling similar goods. After 50 m/yds, the small lane Silom Soi 4 is all bars and outdoor seating. There is a gentle gay scene here at places like **Telephone** and **Sphinx**, see ⑴②, and a small but good all-comers club-bar called **Tapas**.

Little Tokyo

Further along Thanon Silom, Soi Thaniya is the city's **Little Tokyo ❹**, lined with sushi joints and karaoke bars, where hostesses stand outside greeting Japanese tourists with loud choruses of '*Irrashai Mase Dozo!*' (Hello, welcome, please come in). Alternatively, there is a large Irish theme pub on the corner, **O'Reilly's**, and in the middle on the left there is an illicit moonshine stall, discreetly placed beyond the entrance to a car park, where you can buy *ya dong* (pickled medicines) and possibly virility drinks such as *Phaya Chang Sarn* (Power of the Great Elephant). On the right towards the end of Soi Thaniya, swing by **The Barbican**, see ⑴③, for more of an East-West vibe.

Food and Drink

① **LE BOUCHON**
37/17 Patpong Soi 2; tel: 0 2234 9109; Mon–Sat noon–3pm, daily 6.30–11pm; $$$
An atmospheric bistro with just seven tables, popular with local Francophiles for simple home cooking presented on a blackboard menu. Have an aperitif at the bar while you wait for a seat.

② **SPHINX**
100 Silom Soi 4; tel: 0 2234 7249; daily 6pm–1am; $–$$
This gay bar is also frequented by straights for its menu of well-prepared Thai and Western food. Good choices include northern specialities *laab* and *khao soy*. Serves late and has outside tables.

③ **THE BARBICAN**
9/4–5 Soi Thaniya; tel: 0 2233 4141-2; daily 11am–2am; $$
This split-level pub/wine bar is decked out in leather, teak and brushed concrete, and serves good Western and Thai food; friendly atmosphere, and occasional DJ nights.

BANGLAMPHU

After learning at Democracy Monument about the coup that toppled absolute monarchy, stroll past Bangkok's oldest wooden building, take a riverside walk through Santichaiprakarn Park, and check out the nightlife on the Khao San Road, one of the hippest destinations in town.

DISTANCE 3km (2 miles)
TIME A half day
START King Prajadhipok Museum
END Khao San Road
POINTS TO NOTE
Khao San Road is at its liveliest in the evening, so this tour is best started around 2pm. To get to the King Prajadhipok Museum from downtown, hail a taxi or take a river taxi along Khlong Saen Saeb from Pratunam Pier to Tha Saphan Pan Fah.

Most visitors know of the Khao San Road as a famous backpacker enclave, but the scene is also enriched by young bohemian Thais, who help to make Banglamphu one of the most relaxed areas of the city, with a perpetual party atmosphere.

KING PRAJADHIPOK MUSEUM

Start the tour at the **King Prajadhipok Museum ❶** (2 Thanon Lan Luang; tel: 0 2280 3413/4; Tue–Sun 9am–4pm; charge), and learn something of the intrigue behind the end of absolute

Below: Wat Bowoniwet; and stairway detail.

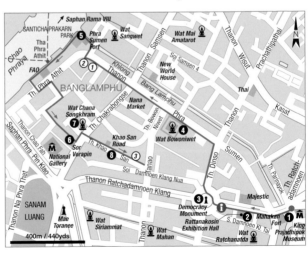

Above from far left:
Wat Bowoniwet;
bustling Khao San
Road; the Democracy
Monument.

monarchy in 1932, when Prajadhipok (Rama VII, 1925–35) was king. The museum examines the king's life through photos, official documents, personal effects and audio-visual displays. They cover his school days at Eton and his coronation, plus significant public works such as construction of Memorial Bridge. The king abdicated in 1935 and lived the rest of his life in England. The white neoclassical building used to be the John Sampson Store, an early Bangkok purveyor of Western clothes.

THE RATTANAKOSIN EXHIBITION HALL

From the museum walk west on Thanon Ratchadamnoen Klang, crossing the bridge which has remnants of the walls of Mahakan Fort and Thanon Maha Chai. After 50m/yds is the **Rattanakosin Exhibition Hall ❷** (100 Thanon Ratchadamnoen Klang; tel: 0 2621 0044; Tue-Fri 11am–8pm, Sat–Sun 10am–8pm; charge), which opened in 2010. It displays the official history of the area from a mainly royal perspective, with multimedia displays including architecture, traditional arts and the Grand Palace. Visitors also have the chance to learn some *khon* masked dance and puppetry skills.

DEMOCRACY MONUMENT

From the Exhibition Hall continue west for 100m/yds to the **Democracy Monument ❸** in the centre of the road. Dedicated to the 1932 coup that led to constitutional monarchy, the central plinth, surrounded by four angular pillars, represents the country's first Constitution, protected by the army, navy, police and air force. The bas-relief imagery at the base was crafted by Italian sculptor Corrado Feroci, who adopted the name Silpa Bhirasi. He founded Silpakorn University and is known as the 'father of modern Thai art'. The images echo the workers' struggles, the iconography of Communist art, although far-left politics have never been strong in Thailand. The monument was the rallying spot for demonstrations in 1973, 1976, 1992 and 2010 that led to many civilian deaths.

WAT BOWONIWET

Cross Thanon Ratchadamnoen Klang at Democracy Monument into Thanon Dinso. At the end on the left there is a row of shops selling Thai flags, official insignia and photos of royalty, some as large as 3m (10ft), to be used in pageants. You can order flags of other countries here too.

Turn left into Thanon Phra Sumen, where **Wat Bowoniwet ❹** (tel: 0 2281 28313; daily 8am–5pm; free) sits 50m/yds on the left at No. 248. King Rama IX was ordained here in 1946, and King Rama IV was once the abbot. The interior is famous for murals painted by a monk called Krua In Khong, regarded as Thailand's first artist to work with perspective. The temple contains Thailand's second Buddhist University, along with Wat Mahathat *(see p.31)*. Opposite the temple is Pratu Wang Kao, one of the old city gates.

Development Plan
The government
has an on-off
Ratchadamnoen-
Champs-Elysées Plan,
which would see an
underground walkway
to the Democracy
Monument, along
with up-market shops
and hotels. The
Champs-Elysées was
the original model for
Ratchadamnoen when
it was constructed in
1899 under the reign
of King Rama V *(see
margin, p.44)*. The
new plan has been
criticised for poten-
tially harming an
important historical
area and its commu-
nities for the sake of
business interests.

Park Live
Santichaiprakarn Park is the venue for open-air performances, most notably live music during the French-inspired festival La Fête de la Musique in June, and the Bangkok Theatre Festival in November.

Below: King Rama VIII Bridge.

PHRA SUMEN FORT AND KHLONG BANG LAMPHU

Continue along Thanon Phra Sumen and go straight over the crossroads into Thanon Phra Athit. You pass **Primavera** café on the left, see ⑪① and opposite, where the road bends sharply to the left, is **Phra Sumen Fort**. Along with Mahakan Fort, it is all that remains of the original 14 fortresses that protected Old Bangkok.

Just before it, trek a short way up the lane leading to a small bridge for a quick view of **Khlong Bang Lamphu**. This canal was dug by 10,000 Cambodian prisoners in 1783, during the reign of Rama I. It joined Khlong Ong Ang close to the Golden Mount to form the original city moat, called Khlong Rop Krung (Canal Surrounding the City). It is now disused, although you may see

some monitor lizards hunting for food in the coffee-coloured waters. The dark plank structure on stilts to the right is believed to be the oldest wooden building in Bangkok. It was part of the original Wat Sam Chin, built in the Ayutthaya period. The wat was damaged by a fire that spread from a neighbouring noodle stall in 1869, and it was restored as Wat Sangwet. In the 20th century the original wooden building was briefly Thailand's first printing school.

SANTICHAIPRAKARN PARK

Return from the bridge and walk around the back of Phra Sumen Fort into the riverside **Santichaiprakarn Park ❺**, where there are good views of the impressive spans of the King Rama VIII Bridge. If you are hungry at this point, cross the road for **Roti-Mataba**, see ⑪②.

Follow the path past the Thai pavilion. In an enclosure at the water's edge are the six remaining *lamphu* trees that give the area its name, Bang Lamphu (Village of the Lamphu). The path snakes past the trees to the river front, taking you beyond the express boat stops at Tha Phra Athit and the United Nations **FAO** office. You can see the old European-style buildings of the latter through the fence. The structure was originally Maliwan Palace, home to several generations of princes. In World War II it housed the operations rooms for the pro-Allies Seri Thai (Free Thai) Movement.

Food and Drink 🍴

① PRIMAVERA
56 Th Phra Sumen. tel: 0 2281 4718; www.primavera-cafe.com; $–$$
Wood-panelled European-style coffee shop. Top billing on a short menu goes to pizza, along with liver pâté and fried calamari. There's a reasonable choice of ice creams and coffees.

② ROTI-MATABA
136 Thanon Phra Athit; tel: 0 2282 2119; Tue–Sun; $
Dip unleavened *roti* and meat-stuffed *mataba* breads into delicious *massaman* and korma curries of fish, vegetables or meat. There are only a few tables, so be prepared to wait.

③ BRICK BAR
265 Khao San Road; tel: 0 2629 4499; $$
Eat, drink and be entertained. Brick Bar's stage hosts three bands a night, mostly rock, ska, reggae and blues, while the Thai and Western menu includes spicy salads, stir-fries and pizzas.

Towards Wat Chana Songkhram

A little further on is **Old Phra Athit Pier**, now a narrow bar-cum-café. Turn left here to Thanon Phra Athit. Cross the road, turn left, then right after 50m/yds into Soi Chana Songkhram, a short lane where the backpacker milieu begins in earnest with guesthouses, tailors, and travel agents offering cheap buses and flights to Chiang Mai and the islands. Look out on the right-hand side for **Nancy Massage Centre**, where you can learn Thai massage.

At the end, turn right, then first left at the top, following the walls of Wat Chana Songkhram. After 80m/yds enter the alley ahead. At the end on the right is the ringside rear entrance to **Sor Vorapin** ❻ (13 Trok Kasab; tel: 0 2243 3651; daily 8–10.30am, 3–5.30pm), a simple gym offering Muay Thai (kickboxing) lessons. If you turn out to be any good they will even find you fights at local stadiums.

From the gym go up the stairs outside to the right. These will take you through the back door of a café. Once inside, go down the stairs and then out of the front entrance into Thanon Chakrabongse.

WAT CHANA SONGKHRAM

Head a short way northeast along Thanon Chakrabongse for **Wat Chana Songkhram** ❼ (tel: 0 2281 8244; daily 8am–6pm; free) on the left. Ethnic Mon monks worshipped at this temple in its early years when it had a Mon name, Wat Tong Pu. In 1787 King

Rama I prescribed the current name, meaning War Victory Temple, after his brother's success in the Battle of the Nine Armies against the Burmese.

KHAO SAN ROAD

Opposite the temple is **Khao San Road** ❽, where homeowners first opened their doors to paying guests in 1982 during the Bangkok Bicentennial. The strip quickly became a legendary stopover for budget travellers on round-the-world trips and achieved wider fame after it featured in the book and film *The Beach* (2000) by Alex Garland and Danny Boyle respectively.

In the late 1990s, after local film and TV companies began using the street as a location, young Thais craving a sympathetic ambience for their own growing 'indie' lifestyle started opening their own places to hang out in. The result is a mix of Eastern and Western twentysomething culture that stretches over several blocks and is one of the most vibrant areas of the city.

Walking from Thanon Chakrabongse, you pass jugglers, buskers, tattooists, hair-braiders, body-piercers, tarot readers and dealers in fake IDs. There are well-stocked second-hand bookshops, wholesale silver merchants and women from northern hill tribes selling beautiful jewellery. Street-side bars tempt people to linger and watch the world go by, and there are also clubs, including the good live-music venue **Brick Bar**, see ⑪③, at the end of the street on the left.

Above from far left:
Thai Pavilion, Santichaiprakarn Park;
Phra Sumen Fort;
street-side café on
Khao San Road.

Take to the Streets
Khao San Road is where the Thai New Year celebrations (Songkran) are at their best, or worst, depending on your disposition. The area heaves with merry-makers in an orgy of mutual drenching. The authorities both promote it and decry it, having tried in recent years to ban high-pressure water guns, talcum powder (which is smeared on people) and tops with spaghetti straps (because they are thought to encourage inappropriate behaviour).

CHATUCHAK

Reputed to be the biggest flea market in the world, Chatuchak – or JJ, as local people increasingly call it – has pretty much anything you can imagine, from beads and Buddhas to snakes and violins.

Money

At the start of the tour, by the ceramics stall at the end of the first stretch of ring road, look across the car park and you will see a row of banks with ATM machines.

Food and Drink

① FUNTALOP

Section 26, Chatuchak Market; $

This stall's wooden tables are jammed with people eating deep-fried chicken marinated with soy sauce, tamarind and pepper, and *somtam* (spicy green papaya salad). Tables are communal; if there is space just smile and sit down.

Chatuchak Market has an estimated 10,000 stalls that attract 250,000 shoppers each weekend. So if something catches your eye and you get diverted from this overview tour, don't worry, there are treasures around every corner.

LAYOUT

Although the size and bustle of the main market makes navigation confusing, there is a logic to it. The stalls are arranged by themed zones in numbered blocks, each in a grid pattern criss-crossed by alleys called *sois* and *sub sois* (similar to the city's street system). Overhead signs indicate the section number, while addresses are marked above each stall and may read, for example, 23, 301, 4/1, corresponding to the section, stall number, *soi* and *sub soi*.

A wider, mainly pedestrianised ring road offers a quick way to move between sections and breezier respite when the going gets tough and hot.

CERAMICS, PUPPETS AND ESSENTIAL OILS

Start the tour at Kamphaeng Phet Metro Station, and turn left onto the ring road past buskers that might include classical masked dance performers and people playing the Thai xylophone. Food-sellers along the right include **Funtalop**, see ⑪①, if you want a pit-stop or to soak up the scene before you dive in; on the left are books, musical instruments and, at the end, wooden classical Thai statuary. On the opposite corner, beside the

ceramics trader, take the alley immediately on the right (Soi 1), where a stall dispenses essential oils of lemongrass, orchid, lilac, vanilla and so on. Next door is a sandstone outlet with spa-like wall plaques and huge Buddha faces that might enrich your garden.

Past the next alley, a jumble of tapestries make a colourful backdrop for puppets hanging from threads. A few metres further on, **Lek Antiques** displays porcelain jars, fishbone chess sets and red-leather Chinese boxes.

BAGS, BLOUSES AND BEADS

Turn left into Soi 1/6, where the small café-bar **Viva** serves coffee, tea and beer, with bands playing from 6pm as the market closes down. Carry on to the end, past scarves and shawls at **Rattanaporn**, and across Soi 2 into the alley opposite. A few metres down, long-haired Kai sells handmade satchels with original designs based on hill-tribe patterns, and ethnic jewellery from Tibet and Nepal.

Walk on and turn left at Soi 3. **Nayana**, on the right, has loose white-cotton shirts and blouses with mandarin collars and traditional Thai detailing. Next door is **Ta**, selling chains and beads of amethyst, buffalo bone and sea bamboo for making your own jewellery.

OPIUM WEIGHTS AND FILM POSTERS

Turn right here and right again at Soi 4. At the corner of Sub Soi 7 a musty stall sells bronze and copper bowls, temple bells, gongs and tiny animal-shaped opium weights from Burma. At the end of Soi 4, Chatuchak's **central square** is ringed by stalls mainly selling clothes, most of which are Thai sizes, and just down on the right there's a no-name massage stall where you can get relief for those aching feet from B150.

POP T-SHIRTS AND REVOLUTION

Across the square, in Section 23, Soi 32, a bunch of T-shirt stalls includes

Shopping Tactics

It is acceptable to bargain for everything, even if the price looks fixed. Watching others shop, particularly Thais, who will mostly get a better price, may give you an idea of how low you can go. Buy water to carry with you – there are plenty of outlets selling it on the ring road – and keep your valuables close by: as with any crowded place, there are pickpockets on the prowl.

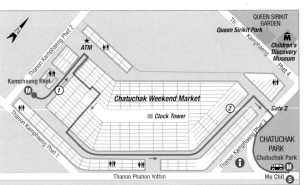

Below: fried seafood.

Antiques

Many stalls will claim to sell antiques, but unless you know what you are doing it is best to treat such claims with a pinch of salt. Evaluate your buys according to what they are worth to you, not as possible investments.

Japanese and superhero designs at Work, tucked down 32/6 on the left, and several easy-come-easy-go stalls with original motifs, from robots to romantic fantasy. At the corner of 31/3 on the left is **Red Star House**, where designer Kris sells revolutionary souvenirs. He is a fervent 'anti-imperialist' and very happy to debate political issues as he tries to sell you a Che Guevara cigarette case.

COWBOYS AND FASHION

At the end of Soi 32 is the pedestrian ring road. Turn left, passing stalls loaded with hats, plants and trousers, and by the entrance to Section 21 you will see a drinks stand, known simply as **Shop**

Coke. Perch here on a plastic stool and have a refreshing coconut juice directly from the shell. Beside Section 12 is **The Cowboy Shop**, recognisable by the wizened Thai hillbillies in Stetsons playing banjos outside. When the owner, Aek, is not flogging rhinestone boots and vintage Nashville shirts, he hangs out at the OK Corral in Khao Yai National Park.

Just by Section 8 is the small **Jeed-Jard** café, see ⑪②, and next door is **Ga Dee Nang** with cutesy tops and fishermen's trousers adorned with vintage Thai and Chinese designs.

ART OF ALL KINDS

When you get to Gate 2 on your right, diagonally opposite to the left you will see the stalls of several **shipping agents**, from where you can ship home all the goodies you have just bought. The section behind is full of art, from young and punky to temple-style wood panels.

Leave by Gate 2, turn right past the grilled seafood stalls, bear left at the fork, then left again at the main road. Mo Chit Skytrain Station is 150m/yds ahead, with Chatuchak Park Metro-Station to the left.

Outside the Market

Chatuchak is ever-expanding, with market stalls spilling onto the surrounding streets and neighbouring land. The road-side sellers on Thanon Phahon Yothin, towards Saphan Khwai Sky-train station, do a roaring trade in Buddhist amulets, while the warehouse outlets on the opposite side of Thanon Kamphaeng Phet 2 have forests of furniture. On Thanon Kamphaeng Phet 1, opposite Kamphaeng Phet Station, is Or Tor Kor, possibly Bangkok's best fresh-produce market, selling lots of regional foods that are difficult to find in the rest of the city. Next to Chatuchak Market, close to Gate 2, is Chatuchak Park (Thanon Pahonyothin; tel: 0 2272 4575), which contains the Rail Hall of Fame and a butterfly garden. Adjacent is Queen Sirikit Park, with a botanical garden; and the Children's Discovery Museum (Thanon Kamphaeng Phet 4; tel: 0 2615 7333; charge), containing a playground and terrific inter-active displays, and offering classes in subjects such as cooking, music and car maintenance.

Food and Drink 🍴
② JEED-JARD
Section 8, Soi 17/1, Chatuchak Market; $
This small, clean café has cooling fans and sells northeastern food like spicy pork sausage, fried chicken with fiery mango salad, and the region's preferred sticky rice.

NONTHABURI &
KO KRET

*An hour's boat ride north of the city is a beautiful country temple and
a small community of ethnic Mon, who make exquisite pottery
and cook traditional foods on an island with no cars.*

The provincial riverside town of Nonthaburi is just 10km (6 miles) north of Bangkok, but feels a world away from the hectic city.

Having caught an express boat from downtown, disembark at the final pier, Nonthaburi, and take a ferry across the river where tuk tuks are lined up waiting for fares. Negotiate a price with the driver to take you to Wat Chaloem Phra Kiet, wait for you and bring you back to the pier; it should cost around B50.

WAT CHALOEM PHRA KIET

Five minutes away, **Wat Chaloem Phra Kiet ❶** (Bang Sri Muang; tel: 0 2446 4035; daily 8.30am–5pm; free) sits behind ramparts that are a legacy of the fort that was built on the site in the reign of King Narai the Great (1656–88), during the Ayutthaya period. King Rama III (1824–51) constructed the wat, in part from the old fort walls, to honour his mother and grandparents.

From the road, you enter by the back door. Pass through a peaceful garden of ornamental trees to the beautiful *bot* (ordination hall), which is notable for a Chinese-earthenware mosaic roof designed as flowers in purple, red and gold. The floor inside is decorated with

---

DISTANCE 20km (12½ miles)
TIME A leisurely day
START/END Bangkok
POINTS TO NOTE
You can start the tour from any convenient express boat pier, such as Tha Saphan Taksin. The journey takes about one hour. To reach Ko Kret, catch a river taxi from Nonthaburi to the landing pier in Pakret, then take the ferry.

---

mirrored tiles, the wooden windows have gold-leaf paintings of bucolic scenes, and there is a large copper seated Buddha. Also in the compound are a tall white *chedi* and two *viharn* (prayer halls).

This is a river-front temple; pass through the gateway beside the *bot* and you will come to a compound of rain trees with refreshment stalls and twin wooden *salas* (open-walled pavilions) from which to enjoy the view.

Lunch

Return to the ferry boat pier and cross back over the river to Nonthaburi Pier. If you walk to the street outside, there are clean toilets a short way to the left,

Above from far left:
The Cowboy Shop;
boat to Nonthaburi.

The Land Route
You can also go from Bangkok to Pakret by taxi. It costs about B200 including expressway tolls.

Below: Wat Chaloem Phra Kiet.

Above from left:
Mon pottery in Ko Kret; reclining Buddha and exterior view, Wat Poramaiyikawat.

and 100m/yds to the right is the **Rim Fung** floating restaurant, see ⑪①, which makes a good stop for lunch. Ahead of you is the market town of **Nonthaburi**, which is famous for its fruit. The durian is particularly notorious: the fruit's hard, spiky exterior hides creamy flesh with an aroma like a ripe sewer, making it one of the strangest food experiences on earth.

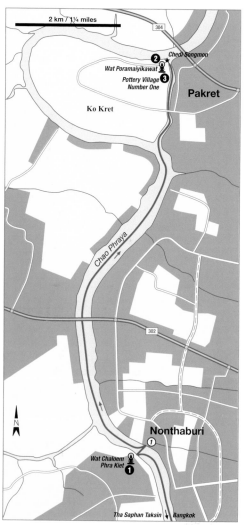

KO KRET

From Nonthaburi Pier catch a river taxi to Pakret (about a 20-minute journey); the half-size longtail boats make for a high-powered, exhilarating and bumpy ride. The return trip is around B800 per boat, but they seat eight, so you can cut the price by sharing with other people.

From here take a two-minute ferry ride to **Ko Kret**, a 4 sq km (1 sq mile) island created during the Ayutthaya period, when the Lat Kret Noe canal was built to shorten the journey to the old capital. It is populated by Mon, a people of Indo-Burmese origin, some of whom were given refuge here when they fled the kingdom of Pegu, in Burma, after the Burmese king Alaungpaya destroyed it in 1757.

A single road, running in a loop around the island, links seven small communities, which although largely assimilated into Thai culture retain aspects of the Mon way of life. This, and the tranquil rural atmosphere, has made the island a regular destination for Thai tourists, especially at weekends.

Wat Poramaiyikawat

The ferry stops beside **Wat Poramaiyikawat** ❷ (Moo 7; tel: 0 2584 5120; Mon–Fri 1–4pm, Sat–Sun 9am–5pm; free), which contains a full set of Mon-language Buddhist *Tripi-*

taka (scriptures), given to the temple by King Rama V. Mon is still studied by monks at the temple, which is possibly the only place on the island where the language is still spoken.

A small **museum** displays old accoutrements of monastic life, including amulets and a *hem* (monk's coffin), as well as the bed of Rama III's daughter, Princess Lamom, which was donated to the temple after her death.

The temple sits in a small **park**, where families picnic under the trees, possibly on food bought at the temple market (weekends only). In a corner is a white stupa called **Chedi Songmon**, which, due to subsidence, leans precariously towards the river. Local legend says that when it eventually falls the local Mon will be able to return to their homeland.

Food Stalls

From the temple, head along the road leading south. Almost immediately you will pass food stalls beside the river, a good place to have a break for a drink or a meal of Mon specialities like *khao chae* (a bowl of various savoury morsels served with chilled, jasmine-infused rice). This has now become a traditional Thai dish, popular in up-market hotels, and eaten mainly as a summer delicacy.

Pottery Village Number One

About 500m/yds from the food stalls is **Pottery Village Number One** ❸ (Moo 1; tel: 08 1989 8229; daily 8am–5pm, workshop weekdays only). Ko Kret is best-known for its Mon pottery

(a Mon water vessel features as Nonthaburi's provincial emblem), which is intricately designed, unglazed and either coloured orange or blackish-grey. The pottery village still has its old-fashioned brick kilns (now superseded by modern ovens), although the traditional method of softening the clay – by using buffaloes to trample it – has been replaced by kneading machines. On weekdays you can see all the processes in action, from clay-slicing to carving, and the owners will be happy to show you around at weekends. A shop sells items such as bowls, incense burners and ornate vases, priced between 100 and several thousand baht. You can also visit a small orchard of exotic fruit trees on the property.

Touring the whole island takes about three hours on foot or half that by bike *(see margin, right)*. It is a satisfying rural escapade, but the pattern of life – temples, orchards and pottery workshops – remains the same, so this is a good place to turn back if you are tired.

Take the ferry back to your river taxi, which will return you to Nonthaburi Pier from where you can catch an express boat back to Bangkok.

Ko Kret Transport

Most people get around Ko Kret either on foot or bicycle, which can be hired for B40 a day at various spots en route. In many places the path is only wide enough for two people abreast, so progress is at a gentle pace. Quicker options are motorbike taxis (there are no cars on the island) or river taxis, which cost about B20 to hop between piers.

Food and Drink 🍴

① RIM FUNG

235/2 Thanon Pracharat, Nonthaburi; tel: 0 2525 1742; daily 11am–10pm; $

This wooden floating restaurant offers a menu that includes marinated hot-plate chicken, whole catfish and fried frogs, served with spicy salads. In the background Thai country music accompanies your meal.

Below: leaning Chedi Songmon.

12

WEST OF BANGKOK

The countryside west of the capital teems with historical sights, from the country's oldest city and the world's largest Buddhist monument to fascinating ceramic workshops and traditional floating markets.

Short on Time
You can do this trip in one day, but you need to leave Bangkok by 6.30am to catch the Floating Market at its best. Then, either continue on to Rama II Memorial Park and the second part of the tour, or do the first part in reverse.

DISTANCE 200km (126 miles)
TIME Two days *(see left)*
START/END Bangkok
POINTS TO NOTE
Although individual points on this tour are accessible by public transport, it is a fiddly journey, so it is far better to hire a car *(see p.110)*. Leave Bangkok along Highway 4, which starts on the west side of town at the King Taksin Monument in Thonburi.

Food and Drink 🍴
① CHEDI SQUARE FOOD STALLS
Thanon Khwa Phra; $
There is a variety of food stalls opposite the *chedi*, where along with regular Thai dishes you will find local specialities such as pink pomelos and *khao lam* (black beans, palm sugar and sticky rice grilled in tubes of hollow bamboo).

Below: bamboo dance demonstration at the Rose Garden.

Once you get past the city's main suburbs, life west of the capital slows to a rural pace. People tend the orchards and farms that supply Bangkok with its fruit, flowers and vegetables. So it is fitting that this tour begins at a site dedicated to preserving plant life and Thailand's traditional customs.

ROSE GARDEN

After about an hour's drive from Bangkok you see signs on the left for the **Rose Garden** ❶ (Km 32, Thanon Phetkasem; tel: 0 3432 2588; www.rose gardenriverside.com; daily 8am–5pm; charge). These 28-hectare (70-acre) grounds nestled in an elbow of the Nakornchaisri River are a big weekend attraction for families fascinated by the wealth of Thai culture and exotic flora.

The lawns are peppered with herb gardens, mahogany, banana and flame trees, and flower beds with resplendent orchids and a variety of rare species. The owners have reconstructed antique wooden houses transported from upcountry and arranged them around a lake. Two daily cultural shows (charge) include morning demonstrations of Thai boxing, rice farming, traditional cooking and even elephant training. In the afternoon there is folk dancing and music. The Rose Garden has restaurants and a hotel on site if you want to linger.

NAKHON PATHOM

Come out of the Rose Garden and head west along Highway 4 for 20km (12 miles), then follow signs to **Nakhon Pathom**, which is popularly referred to as Thailand's oldest city.

Phra Pathom Chedi

Drive along Thanon Tesa, and after 2km (1¼ miles) the town's most noteworthy site, **Phra Pathom Chedi** ❷ (Thanon Khwa Phra; tel: 0 3424 2143; daily 6am–6pm; charge), looms into view – at 127m (417ft) it is the tallest Buddhist monument in the world. At the end of the road turn left, then right at the lights and into the main entrance of the *chedi* on the right.

Indian-style Buddhist artefacts found here have been used to date the site to around 150BC, and conjecture that the city was the capital of ancient lands known as *Suvarnabhum*. Later, from the 6th–11th centuries, Nakhon Pathom was the centre of Dvaravati, an affiliation of city-states in what is now western Thailand, populated by ethnic Mon, with Nakhon Pathom at its centre. There has been a *chedi* on this site since the 6th century, although the original was devastated in a Burmese attack in 1057 and lay in ruins until Rama IV built a new one over the remains in 1860. He constructed a replica of the original a few metres to the south.

The temple that surrounds the *chedi* is one of the most important in Thailand. It has four *viharns* (prayer halls) marking the cardinal compass points, each with a Buddha image. The northernmost, containing a standing Buddha, holds the ashes of Rama VI (1910–25). Leading off the corridors directly around the *chedi* are classrooms for novice monks, while the outer terraces are notable for Chinese statuary and a large reclining Buddha.

You can buy lunch at the **Chedi Square food stalls**, see ⑪①. This space is also used for traditional dance performances, and in an adjacent park each November people celebrate the end of the rainy season during the famous Loy Krathong festival.

Above from far left: Buddha and gold-leaf offerings, Phra Pathom Chedi; umbrella painting, the Rose Garden.

Below: towering Phra Pathom Chedi.

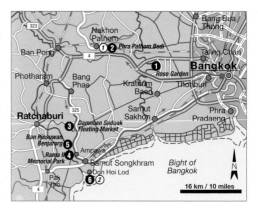

Chedi Museum

The **Phra Pathom Chedi National Museum** (tel: 0 3424 2500; Wed–Sun 9am–4pm; charge), located on the edge of the square to the right of the *chedi*, has the remains of Buddha images and stone carvings from the Dvaravati period.

Overnight Stop

Leaving the *chedi*, turn right along Thanon Khwa Phra, then left at the lights, opposite Silpakorn University. At the top turn right on Highway 4, and stay on this road following signs for Ratchaburi (Ratburi) for 17km (10 miles) before turning left (south) on Route 325 towards Damnoen Saduak, which is about 25km (15 miles) away.

After about 22km (13 miles) look for signs on the right for **Baan Sukchoke Country Resort** *(see p.115)*, a pleasant place to spend the night. It has a restaurant with dishes like 'fried crab narrow dirt mine' presumably named using a Google translation. In the morning, to get to the market, turn right and drive for about 2km (1¼ miles) into town.

FLOATING MARKET

The area southwest of Bangkok is laced with rivers and canals, and the surrounding countryside bursts with produce grown on farmland and in orchards. Traditionally, smallholders would take their wares by boat to local floating markets and sell them directly, while still bobbing on the water. The canal networks ran all the way to Bangkok, and you can still travel the full distance to the capital in this way today.

Over the last 30 years, however, roads have superseded waterways, the few remaining markets have become tourist attractions, and the traders, in their wide-brimmed hats, are poster girls for ad campaigns. That said, if you get to the most famous floating market at **Damnoen Saduak** ❸ before 9am when the tour coaches arrive, this is still a fun and largely faithful dip into traditional Thai culture.

Exploring the Market

As you reach Damnoen Saduak go over the flyover, then turn right at the lights under the ornate Thai-style gateway into the small lane leading to the market. You can drive along it all the way to the bridge and view proceedings from dry land, but far more pleasant is to stop at one of the tour operators advertised at the roadside, where for around B300 an hour you can hire a boat seating six people. The driver will inevitably try to stop at waterside shops, where there will be a gentle hassle to sell you things. Just tell him if you would rather miss out these detours.

Every day the main market mostly sells foodstuffs, such as fruit, spices, vegetables and one-plate dishes cooked on board the boats, although around a corner a **second canal section** has handicrafts, trinkets, T-shirts and other souvenirs. As usual, haggle a price for everything. Your boat driver will also take you beyond the market and into the countryside if you ask.

Local Boy
King Rama II (1809–24), who was born in Amphawa, is known as the poet king. His famous *Boat Songs* were often odes to his favourite foods, such as the paean to *latiang*, a refined egg net used to wrap minced delicacies: 'Latiang is like the pillow on which I dream, and the heavens from which I rise…'

RAMA II MEMORIAL PARK

Leave town by turning right (south) onto Route 325 for about 10km (6 miles), then turn right towards the cosy little village of **Amphawa**, which has its own floating market (Fri–Sun pm only). Go over the bridge, then just after the large white temple turn left into **Rama II Memorial Park ❹** (Thanon Mae Klong Bang Nok Kwaek; tel: 0 3475 1666; daily 6.30am–5pm; charge). As well as botanical gardens, the park has traditional Thai buildings housing an ethnological museum depicting early Rattanakosin-period lifestyles and a display of musical instruments. A fair here every February celebrates Thai music, dance and drama.

BENJARONG WORKSHOP

Go back to Route 325 and turn left, then left again after 100m/yds. Almost immediately on the right is **Ban Pinsuwan Benjarong ❺** (32/1 Moo 7, Bangchang; tel: 0 3475 1322; daily 8am–noon, 1–5pm; workshop closed Sun pm). The owner of this small family workshop, Virat Pinsuwan, is an antiques restorer who was inspired to make Benjarong pieces *(see p.18)* using traditional designs. He has become so successful that orders take eight months to fill. Take a tour, watch craftsmen work, and buy from a small selection of items. A tiny teacup and saucer will cost around B1,200, but considering they take three days to make, and are exquisite, this may well be a bargain. There is also a small ceramics museum.

DON HOI LOT

Go back to Route 325, turn left and do a U-turn after 100m/yds. This road runs all the way to the town of Samut Songkhram, from where the nearby Don Hoi Lot is an ideal place to lunch before heading back to Bangkok.

At the end of Route 325 turn right and follow the main road through town until it brings you onto Rama II Road. Go over the bridge, which follows a long loop onto Highway 35. After 2km (1¼ miles) leave the highway following signs to Don Hoi Lot, then do a U-turn after 100m/yds.

About 6km (4 miles) further on is **Don Hoi Lot ❻**, where seafood stalls line the road and restaurants jut out on wooden piers into the Mae Khlong River Delta. Stop at **Khun Pao Restaurant**, see ⑪②, where you can try the *hoi lot* (razor clams) that give the area its name. If you are lucky and the water is low, you will see the fossilised remains of the clams sticking out of the mud close to shore.

To return to Bangkok, go back to Highway 35 and do a U-turn according to the signs. The drive is about one hour.

(see p.18)

Food and Drink

② KHUN PAO RESTAURANT
1/3 Moo 4, Don Hoi Lot; tel: 0 3472 3703; $–$$
A rustic spot overlooking the Mae Khlong River Delta. The speciality is seafood, including the celebrated *hoi lot* (razor clams), unappetisingly referred to as 'worm shells' on the menu. Delicious nevertheless.

Above from far left: snapshots of Damnoen Saduak Floating Market.

Standout Ceramics
Notable pottery styles on sale at Ban Pinsuwan Benjarong include: Sangkhalok, which dates to the Sukhothai period (from c.1294), and is normally one solid colour; Benjarong, which must contain at least five colours and was prevalent in Ayutthaya from 1656; and Lai Kram, which are blue-on-white designs that started in the fourth reign of the Rattanakosin era (from 1851).

13 KANCHANABURI

Drive west to visit a laid-back town with a dark history: it was here that the Bridge on the River Kwai and 'Death Railway' were built during World War II. Afterwards, lighten the mood with a swim in a waterfall, a shopping trip for sapphires, or a visit to the big cats at the Tiger Temple.

Above: only the eight curved sections of the Bridge on the River Kwai are original; the rest of it was rebuilt after World War II.

DISTANCE Bangkok to Kanchanaburi: 130km (75 miles); Kanchanaburi tour: 7.25km (4½ miles)

TIME One or two days

START Bridge on the River Kwai

END Kanchanaburi War Cemetery

POINTS TO NOTE

It is best to hire a car to get to Kanchanaburi. Leave Bangkok west on Highway 4, head 10km (6 miles) past Nakhon Pathom, then follow Route 323 to Kanchanaburi. If you go by train or bus, you can get around town by tuk tuk or *songthaew* (open-backed taxi vans) for around B30 a go, or hire motorbikes and bicycles along River Kwai Road.

The tour can be done as a busy day trip; alternatively, stay overnight and explore Erawan National Park on day two. For overnight options, see p.81.

Death Railway

Three trains run daily from the bridge, on a sheer-drop narrow track past jungle and limestone cliffs to the terminus at Nam Tok about two hours away, where you can swim in a nearby waterfall during the rainy season. Return journeys start around two hours later. Break your journey by visiting the Khmer ruins at Muang Singh Historical Park (tel: 0 3459 1122; daily 9am–4.30pm; charge); alight at Tha Kilen Station, from where you can take a *songthaew* to the ruins.

BRIDGE ON THE RIVER KWAI

Kanchanaburi is well worth the two-to three-hour drive it takes to get there. The town is famous as the location of the **Bridge on the River Kwai ❶**, part of the 'Death Railway' built by prisoners of the occupying Japanese forces in World War II. The story of how some 16,000 Allied POWs and up to 100,000 Asian slave labourers died during the construction was told in the 1957 film *Bridge on the River Kwai*, starring Alec Guinness. Parts of the bridge are original, but the central arches were rebuilt following Allied bombing in the war. Period steam trains are parked close by, with more at the main railway station on Saeng Chuto Road.

You can walk across the bridge, but gaps in the planking reveal long drops into the river, so people have to shuffle carefully around each other on the firm central plates between the tracks. Niches between the spans provide a refuge in case a rare train happens along.

The railway was built to link what was then Burma to Japanese positions in the rest of Asia, both as a supply route and to exploit the country's natural resources. It is said that one prisoner died for every sleeper laid.

WORLD WAR II MUSEUM

From the bridge walk 50m/yds along River Kwai Road, past the shops, to reach the **World War II Museum ❷** (395–403 River Kwai Road; tel: 0 3451 2596; daily 7am–6pm; charge) on the right. Despite its name, this

eccentric collection is in many ways a vanity project for the family that owns it; one of the two buildings here has a celebration of the family achievements on the top floor. The rest includes artefacts from Thai history and an art collection as well as war-related items. There are the remains of a wooden footbridge built by prisoners to cross the river, plus weapons and vehicles. Despite a slightly tacky ambience and poorly labelled exhibits, this is still an entertaining diversion. On the road next to the museum is a Japanese War Memorial Shrine.

LUNCH STOP

Leaving the museum, drive away from the bridge along River Kwai Road, which bends left after 1.5km (1 mile) at **Apple's Guesthouse** (52 Rong Heeb Oay Road; tel: 0 3451 2017; www. applenoi-kanchanaburi.com; closed for lunch), a good place to return to for dinner. Then bear right where the road forks and drive for another 150m/yds, where the road narrows between rows of low shops. At the small crossroads turn right. At the lights bear left (not over the bridge), then continue straight ahead again at the next lights, where you will come to a long stretch of river front lined with floating restaurants and cafés. Although much of the food is only so-so, this is an atmospheric place to stop off for lunch; try **Tara Buree**, see ①① *(p.81)*. You will find boats for hire too, if you want a river trip. Continue past the restaurants up the hill to the end and turn right into Chaichumpol Road.

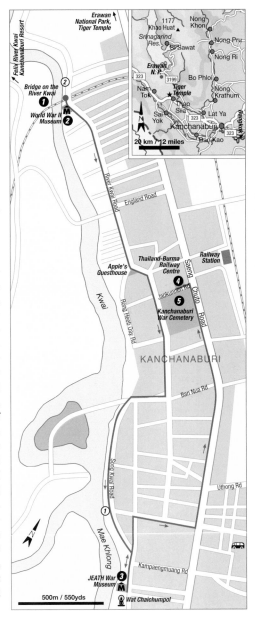

Blue Sapphires

Kanchanaburi is well known for blue sapphires, which are mined north of town in Bo Phloi. You can buy them in the small shopping plaza near the River Kwai Bridge, but as this is a tourist area prices are inflated and you will need to bargain hard for a good deal. To avoid scams it is best to find shops with licences displayed on the wall and avoid the street touts. If you want to see how a sapphire factory works, the The Blue Ploy (11 Saeng Chuto Road 11; tel: 08 1856 2570) is open to visitors.

JEATH WAR MUSEUM

After another 500m/yds you will come to a temple at the top which is called Wat Chaichumpol. Adjacent to it is the **JEATH War Museum ❸** (tel: 0 3451 5203; daily 8am–6pm; charge), which was founded in 1977 by a monk called Phra Theppanyasuthee, who has since become abbot of the temple. The museum is named after the countries whose dead it is intended to commemorate: Japan, England, America, Australia, Thailand and Holland. The building – which is modelled on one of the bamboo huts in which prisoners of war were incarcerated – contains newspaper clippings, personal items such as photographs and clothes, and drawings by ex-prisoners depicting their life in the camps.

THAILAND–BURMA RAILWAY CENTRE

Head back along Thanon Chaichumpol, and then turn right through the monumental white city gates. Beyond the city pillar, take a left at the traffic lights along the Saeng Chuto Road, then left again after 2km (1¼ miles) into Jaokunnen Road, where the **Thailand–Burma Railway Centre ❹** (tel: 0 3451 2721; www.tbrconline.com; daily 9am–5pm; charge) is situated 50m/yds on the right at No. 73.

This is the latest of Kanchanaburi's war-related museums and although in more sterile surroundings than its rivals, it benefits from better-labelled and more coherent displays. It also has a more professional retail operation, selling everything from books on the Death Railway to souvenir caps and key chains.

The two-floor exhibition space starts with a timeline and useful maps plotting Japanese expansion in Asia and then moves through videos, models and photos showing the prisoners' living and working conditions. During a push to complete the railway quickly, increased labour hours and poor nutrition caused the deaths of 7,000 prisoners in a five-month period to October 1943. A model of a hospital hut, with dioramas of amputations being performed, details the medical staff's struggles to cope with equipment improvised from found objects such as old bicycles.

On the second floor exhibits include moving personal items such as diary entries and letters from home. A café on site has snack meals and drinks.

The Tiger Temple

Wat Pa Luanta Bua Yannasampanno, which is better-known as the Tiger Temple (Km 21, Route 323; tel: 0 3453 1557; daily 8.30am–5.30pm; charge), is a major tourist draw one hour out of town on the road west. In 1999 the abbot of this forest monastery adopted a couple of tiger cubs abandoned in the wild, and a breeding programme has seen the animals increase in number to double figures. They are let out of their cages daily, at around 3pm, when visitors can view and, in some cases, pat them.

The temple is a very popular attraction, but controversial too, with critics claiming mistreatment and illegal trading of animals. Also, entrance charges have steadily risen (to B600 at the time of writing), leading to claims of profiteering, which is deemed unsuitable for a Buddhist temple.

KANCHANABURI
WAR CEMETERY

Opposite the museum is the **Kancha-naburi War Cemetery** ❺, where the 7,000 Australian, British and Dutch casualties of the Death Railway are buried or commemorated (the US dead have been repatriated). Despite the tourist buses, the cemetery retains its serenity, and, having seen the museum's displays that show how the men lived their final days, it can be very moving.

OPTIONAL SECOND DAY

From here you can either head back to Bangkok or stay overnight to explore some of Kanchanaburi's natural attractions the next day. Options include **Apple's Guesthouse** *(see p.79)* or any of the budget accommodation found along the River Kwai Road, or the **Felix River Kwai Kanchanaburi Resort**, which has good river-view rooms *(see p.115)*. The **Keereetara Restaurant**, see ⑪②, situated close to the bridge, is a lovely spot for dinner.

Erawan National Park

Depending on how much you want to see, day two could be long, so start as early as you can. Leave Kanchanaburi, heading northwest for 65km (40 miles) along Route 3199 until you come to the main entrance of **Erawan National Park** (tel: 0 3457 4222; www.dnp.go.th; daily 8am–4.30pm; charge). There are also buses from Kanchanaburi that drop you at Erawan Village. From

there, take a *songthaew* to the park entrance 2km (1¼ miles) away.

There are cafés close to the entrance selling Thai food, and a Visitor Centre with information on the park's attractions, of which the main one is the **Erawan Waterfall**. It has seven tiers, so there are lots of stopping points if you can't make it all the way to the top (a two-hour trek). The park is named after the loftiest point, which is said to resemble Erawan, the three-headed elephant from Hindu mythology. The falls are at their best during and after the rainy season, when water levels are highest and it is possible to enjoy a refreshing swim.

Take water and food with you, and take your time – remember, you have to walk back down again. From Erawan retrace your route to return to Bangkok.

Food and Drink 🍽

① TARA BUREE
48 Song Kwai Road; tel: 0 3451 2944; $–$$
This floating restaurant juts into the river on several pontoons. The view compensates for the basic standard of dishes such as deep-fried prawns with garlic and steamed sea bass with lemon sauce.

② KEEREETARA RESTAURANT
43/1 River Kwai Road; tel: 0 3462 4093; $$
A stylish boutique restaurant with mock Sukhothai-era pillars and detailing. Best to sit on the atmospheric riverside terraces to enjoy a range of dishes including the speciality: snakefish with spicy salad.

Above from far left: JEATH War Museum; sapphires are mined in Kanchanaburi; War Cemetery.

Below: Erawan Waterfall.

Jungle Treks
Kanchanaburi is the starting point for a rich variety of attractions in this largely unspoilt region, and with more time you could happily spend a week trekking, rafting and visiting tribal villages in several national parks. The local guide shops on River Kwai Road all have a wide range of itineraries, from day trips to week-long jungle treks.

SAMUT PRAKAN

Just south of Bangkok are two extraordinary museum projects that preserve Thai heritage: one housed inside a giant three-headed elephant, the other a replica of the whole country, replete with life-size temples and palaces.

DISTANCE Bangkok to Erawan Museum: 20km (12 miles)
TIME A full day
START Erawan Museum
END The Ancient City
POINTS TO NOTE
Take Thanon Sukhumvit to Soi 117, then follow signs to Thanon Kanchanapisek. Turn left towards Bangna and U-turn under the bridge. The Erawan Museum is on the left. For the Ancient City, head left (south) on Thanon Sukhumvit. At Pak Nam turn left. The Ancient City is on the left at Km 33.

Alternatively, bus 511 (air conditioned) goes from Ekamai Bus Station, stopping at Erawan Museum and Pak Nam, where you change to minibus No. 36 to the Ancient City.

Crocodile Shoes
If you would like a break from hard heritage, the nearby Samut Prakan Crocodile Farm (555 Moo 7, Tai Baan, Samut Prakan; tel: 0 2387 0020; daily 7am–6pm; charge) is reputed to be the biggest in the world. It has croc wrestling, elephant shows and a nice line in crocodile and fish skin products certified by CITES (Convention on International Trade in Endangered Species).

The road southeast from Bangkok runs close to the Chao Phraya River and the urban sprawl continues with fish factories and packing plants. But the province of Samut Prakan (part of the Bangkok metropolis) has two extraordinary sites.

THE ERAWAN MUSEUM

The **Erawan Museum** ❶ (Sukhumvit Soi 119; tel: 0 2371 3135; www.erawan-museum.com; daily 8am–5pm; charge)

is housed in an extraordinary 43m (141ft) high three-headed elephant that represents Erawan, the animal ridden by the god Indra in Hindu mythology. It was created by businessman and philanthropist Lek Viriyaphant, whose other projects include the Ancient City, below, and the Sanctuary of Truth, in Pattaya *(see p.94)*.

The museum is divided into three sections. The basement 'Underworld' contains mainly Chinese and Thai pieces from the founder's private antiques collection. The middle section 'Earth' has a stained-glass domed ceiling and examples of Thai art styles from the country's most celebrated craftsmen. These include stucco work from Phetchaburi, hammered tin plating from Nakhon Si Thammarat and ceramics from Amphawa.

In the hollow interior of the elephant's belly, is 'Heaven', a somewhat odd, hippie-esque purple room decorated with abstract murals, and with antique Buddha statues dating to the Dvaravati period from the 6th–13th centuries AD.

Because the museum contains many Buddha images it has assumed the status of a holy place for many Thais, who make the pilgrimage to a shrine in the gardens to earn merit and pray for good luck.

THE ANCIENT CITY

From the museum, turn left on Thanon Sukhumvit and drive for 11.5km (7 miles) to the **Ancient City** ❷ (Muang Boran; tel: 0 2709 1644/5; www.ancientcity.com; daily 8am–5pm; charge) on the left. The parkland site is loosely shaped to represent Thailand, with more than 100 monuments, palaces and other buildings placed approximately in their correct geographical location. Some are life-size or nearly life-size reproductions or reconstructions of long-lost structures; others are buildings that were relocated here. The result is an educational celebration of Thai history and architecture. And while these may be idealised tableaux, there is not an ounce of Disney about any of it.

It could take around four hours to tour the site, but for highlights head to the Central region, where the centrepiece is a reconstruction of the 15th-century Sanphet Prasat Palace, the main royal residence of the early Ayutthaya period. It was notable at the time because it heralded a new architecture that differed from the earlier Khmer and Sukhothai styles in details such as tapering pillars, pedimented door frames and overlapping roofing. It became known as the Ayutthaya School and was to dominate the landscape well into the Rattanakosin era four centuries later. The palace was completely destroyed when the Burmese sacked Ayutthaya in 1767.

Close by are other replica monuments of the country's rich 'Rice Bowl', such as the beautiful Dusit Maha Prasat Palace and the Phra Kaew Pavilion from the current Grand Palace in Bangkok. The site also has period houses of various styles and mock-ups of regional villages with local crafts for sale. There are small open-air cafés around the grounds serving Thai food, with several near the **Floating Market**, see ⑪①. Aside from the monuments, the park offers a peaceful and secluded environment, particularly if you go mid-week.

Food and Drink 🍴

① FLOATING MARKET

The Ancient City; $

As well as being a fun exhibit, the Floating Market has several small cafés, such as Rim Naam, in waterside wooden *salas*. They sell spicy Thai salads and one-plate dishes like garlic chicken on rice.

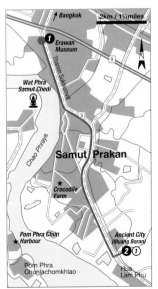

Getting Around

At 129 hectares (320 acres) it is not practical to tour the Ancient City on foot. You can drive around it (charge), rent bicycles or golf carts at the gate, or take a tram tour, which is available with an English-speaking guide (charge).

AYUTTHAYA

Take a trip into Thailand's glorious past, when its ancient capital Ayutthaya had 2,000 golden temples, a population of 1 million, and trade links that stretched from Holland to China.

DISTANCE 76km (48 miles) from Bangkok to Ayutthaya
TIME A full day
START Bang Pa-In
END Ayutthaya
POINTS TO NOTE

There are regular buses and trains, but it is best by car (one hour). From Bangkok take either northbound express route, then follow signs to Bang Pa-In. To see all the sites travel Wed–Sun.

Travelling in Style
Several operators and hotels arrange overnight boat trips to Ayutthaya at various levels of price and comfort. Try www.bangkok-cruises.anantara.com; or www.asian-oasis.com. They are romantic, but you will see less of the city.

Raising Funds
Following the defeat of Ayutthaya, King Taksin was desperate for funds to build the new capital in Thonburi. He authorised treasure hunts in the old city looking for the riches buried by the city's merchants before they fled. Finders were allowed to keep half the loot for themselves.

Ayutthaya is built on an island surrounded by the Chao Phraya, Pa Sak and Lop Buri rivers. It was the fabulously wealthy capital of Thailand (then known as Siam) until it was destroyed in 1767 by invading Burmese armies, who looted and burnt everything in their path. Their city in ruins, the inhabitants fled.

Today those ruins form the Ayutthaya Historical Park, a Unesco World Heritage Site that is tantalisingly suggestive of a cosmopolitan metropolis, with quarters occupied by Chinese, Portuguese, French and countless other nationalities. A pleasant detour en route from Bangkok is the royal retreat of Bang Pa-In.

BANG PA-IN

The lovely palace complex of **Bang Pa-In ①** (tel: 0 3526 1044; www.palaces.thai.net; daily 8am–3.30pm; charge), located 20km (12½ miles) south of Ayutthaya, is arranged around a man-made lake, with many structures on small islands accessed by walkways and bridges. Thailand's rulers came here as long ago as the 17th century, but the current collection of buildings dates from the reigns of kings Rama IV (1851–68) and Rama V (1868–1910). The mix

of Thai, Chinese, Gothic and neo-classical architecture is typical of the latter's reign.

There are buggies available at the main entrance (charge) if you would prefer not to walk around the complex.

Shrines and Pavilions

From the entrance you pass **Ho Hem Monthian Thewarat**, a Khmer-style shrine dedicated to King Prasat Thong of Ayutthaya, who built the original palace here. Ahead to the left in the middle of the lake is **Phra Thinang Aisawan Tippaya-Art** (Divine Seat of Personal Freedom), a magnificent Thai-style pavilion with a spired roof. It is a copy of the Arporn Phimok Prasat in the Grand Palace in Bangkok (see p.28), and contains a bronze statue of King Rama V in military uniform.

Garden of Secured Land

An island hop away is the **Phra Thinang Uthayan Phumisathian** (Garden of Secured Land), where King Rama V preferred to stay. The original two-storey wooden structure, built in 1877, was destroyed by fire in 1938, and this reconstruction was completed in 1996 during the current king's Golden Jubilee year. Only the Gothic water tower remains of the original building.

Other notable features include the classical Chinese **Wehat Chanrun Palace** and, on the other side of the river from the palace and reached by cable car, **Wat Nivet Dhammaparvat**, which with all its Gothic styling and stained-glass windows could be mistaken for a Christian church.

AYUTTHAYA

Leaving Bang Pa-In, turn left from the gate and take the road around the back of the palace along a country lane where traditional houses on stilts line the Chao Phraya River. At the junction turn left and follow signs to **Ayutthaya ②**. At the end of this road turn right towards Route 32, where you turn left and drive after a few kilometres over the Naresuan Bridge into Ayutthaya. The journey from Bang Pa-In takes about 20 minutes.

Ayutthaya Historical Study Centre

Continue along Thanon Rotchana and turn left into the **Ayutthaya Historical Study Centre ④** (Thanon Rotchana; tel: 0 3524 5123; daily 9am–4pm;

Above from far left: Phra Thinang Aisawan Tippaya-Art Pavilion (left) and Bang Pa-In Summer Palace (right); the lotus is commonly used as a prayer offering at Thai temples; Wehat Chanrun Palace.

Below: prang (left) and chedi (right) structures at Wat Chai Wattanaram, situated beside the Chao Phraya River at Ayutthaya.

Getting Around

You can hire Ayutthaya's distinctive bullet-headed tuk tuks and rickshaws at various spots around town, notably at the train station and the car parks at Wat Mahathat and Viharn Phra Mongkhon Bophit. Bicycles are also available (B40 per day), but most are basic and often don't have brakes.

Floating Market and Theatre

Just north of the heritage site, Ayutthaya Klong Sa Bua Floating Market (44 Moo 5 Tambol Klong Sabua; tel: 08 1875 0838; www.ayutthaya floatingmarket.com; Sat–Sun 10am– 5.30pm) opened in 2010. It also has a water theatre (charge) showing traditional folk performances on a stage just below the water's surface to give the impression that the actors are floating.

charge), which is divided into five sections covering the ancient city as capital, state and port, plus traditions and village life. It gives a good introductory overview of this once powerful city. Founded by King Uthong in 1350, Ayutthaya soon took the kingdom of Sukhothai under its rule; the city's influence eventually spread as far as Angkor to the east and Pegu (in what was then Burma) to the west. By the early 1500s the Portuguese, and later the Dutch, British and French, were regular visitors, and Ayutthayan kings engaged Japanese soldiers, Indian men-at-arms and Persian ministers to serve in their retinues.

As the Burmese armies triumphed in 1767, not only were the city's monuments destroyed, but also most official records, in effect ripping the cultural heart from the nation. It was for this reason that King Rama I was committed to creating Bangkok in Ayutthaya's image when he chose it for his new capital in 1782.

Turning left from the centre, near the junction on the right is the **Chao Sam Phraya Museum ®** (Thanon Rotchana; tel: 0 3524 1587; Wed–Sun 9am–4pm; charge), which houses relics discovered around the city, including Buddha images, carvings, stucco work and period art.

Viharn Phra Mongkhon Bophit

Turn right at the top of the road into Thanon Si Sanphet, and go left at the roundabout into Thanon Pha Thon. Turn right just before the bridge over the canal, and after a short way turn into the car park on your right.

The car park leads immediately to a **market** (daily 7am–6pm) which sells crafts, souvenirs and food, and has **food stalls**, see ⑪①, in the central area. The large red temple roof to the rear of the market identifies **Viharn**

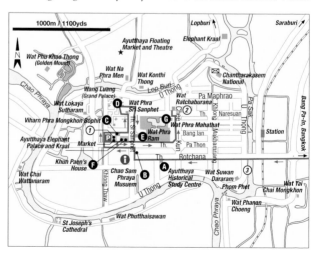

Phra Mongkhon Bophit ⓒ (daily 7am–6.30pm; free). Although itself a new building, the temple is highly venerated for its massive 15th-century bronze Buddha, which had lain unsheltered amid the ruins here for two centuries until the *viharn* (sermon hall) was built to house it in 1956. There are black-and-white photos on the walls showing the statue in its previous condition. While the rest of old Ayutthaya sites are thronged by foreign tourists, this one is a hotspot for Thai worshippers, particularly at weekends.

Wat Phra Sri Sanphet

Take the path on the left of the entrance to the walled **Wat Phra Sri Sanphet** (daily 7am–6.30pm; charge). This royal temple was built in 1491 to honour three 15th-century kings, whose remains are housed in the trio of restored *chedis* standing in a line. These structures have appeared on hundreds of postcards and magazine pages, and are perhaps the most photographed images of Ayutthaya. The Burmese melted the gold off the 16m (52ft) high main standing Buddha image here, and the remains were later removed by King Rama I (and concealed inside Chedi Sri Sanphet at Bangkok's Wat Pho).

Ruined stupas and *chedis* littering the grounds give a glimpse of what the city must have been like when visiting European dignitaries wrote awed accounts of great wealth and 2,000 temple spires clad in gold. At the time its 1 million population was greater than that of London.

Grand Palace

Beyond the wall opposite the wat's entrance is the location of the **Grand Palace** ⓓ (Wang Luang), although only the brick foundations remain (an impressive reproduction of the palace can be see at the Ancient City, *see p.83*). King Borom Trai Lokanath built the royal residence here in 1448 after abandoning King Uthong's original wooden palace (on the site later occupied by Wat Phra Sri Sanphet). The Grand Palace was razed by the Burmese, and the bricks removed to Bangkok to build the city's defensive walls.

Food and Drink 🍴
① FOOD STALLS
Central Market, Viharn Phra Mongkhon Bophit; daily 9am–6pm; $
Diners sit at communal tables ringed by individual vendors selling dishes like Thai omelettes, curries and noodle soups with pork and chicken.

Warrior Queen

One of the most famous heroines of Thai history is Queen Suriyothai, the wife of King Maha Chakapat (1548–69). Legend states that when her husband went to engage the invading Burmese armies in the first year of his reign, Queen Suriyothai disguised herself as a man and rode into battle with him. His elephant wounded, the king found himself in mortal danger, but the queen rode her elephant between him and his attacker and was herself killed. The white-and-gold Chedi Si Suriyothai stands in her honour, overlooking the river on the western edge of the city. In 2001 a movie about her called *Suriyothai* was the most expensive film ever made in Thailand and was a huge box office hit. Francis Ford Coppola edited the US release.

Exploring Further
There is a landing at Chan Kasem Palace where you can rent boats for a leisurely river trip, visiting some of the sites around the edges of the city.

Wat Phra Ram

Facing the palace from Wat Phra Sri Sanphet, turn right along the side of the temple wall and right at the end, past the statue of King Uthong. Ahead to the left is **Wat Phra Ram** ⑤ (daily 8am–6.30pm; charge), which, having been constructed in 1369 by Uthong's son King Ramesuan, is one of the city's oldest temples. It was built on the site of his father's cremation, and has been restored twice. Elephant gates punctuate the old walls, and the central terrace is dominated by a crumbling *prang* (Khmer-style tower) with a gallery of stucco Naga serpents, garudas and Buddha statues.

Khun Paen's House

Come out of Wat Phra Ram into the park opposite. Walk 100m/yds along the right side of the lake and cross over it via the first wooden bridge. On the other side is **Khun Paen's House** ⑥, which,

although empty of furnishings, is a good example of a traditional Thai abode, showing the three separate dwellings of the extended family arranged around a communal veranda for socialising and eating. People habitually ate sitting on the floor, which is the original reason for taking your shoes off when entering a Thai building. It was rebuilt here in 1940, the location of the original city jail. From the house, the view appears to be an idyllic country scene. Many traditional houses in Bangkok, including part of Jim Thompson's home *(see p.60)*, were relocated from Ayutthaya.

Ayutthaya Elephant Palace

Leave the house by the kitchen stairs and turn left. Follow the path to the right, to the entrance of the **Ayutthaya Elephant Palace and Kraal**. You can walk in and join the delighted kids watching the elephant shows at no cost (although the elephants go round

Below: exploring the ruins by elephant.

Food and Drink

② RUEAN ROJJANA
22/13 Thanon Maharat; tel: 0 3532 3765; daily 10am–9pm; $–$$
With some outside tables and traditional triangular cushion seating with wat views, this spot serves tourist favourites like *tom yum goong* and fried chicken with cashew nuts.

③ PAE KRUNG KAO AYUDTHAYA
Km 4, Moo 2, Thanon Authong; tel: 0 3524 1555; daily 10am–9pm; $–$$
This large but cosy restaurant on the river bank is a picturesque spot for curries and spicy salads, or a whole fried fish eaten with dipping sauces.

collecting donations in their trunks after each trick) or take a 20-minute elephant ride to tour nearby sites (B400). The *howdah* seats two adults and a small child. The *mahout* (handler) sits on the elephant's head.

Leave the kraal by the entrance gate, turn right over the footbridge, then walk left through the small car park. Go over the footbridge on the right, and stroll past the small lake. When you cross the next bridge, turn left, then right and you are back in the market. Along with clothes and woven baskets, mounds of fruit and musical instruments, look out for some interesting things to eat like *khanom mor geng*, a dessert of cashew nut pudding topped with fried onions.

Wat Phra Mahathat

Reclaim your car. Turn left from the car park and take the first left back into Thanon Pha Thon. At the second roundabout, turn left into Thanon Maharat, then left again into the car park at **Wat Phra Mahathat G** (daily 7.30am–6.30pm; charge). Souvenir shops here mark this as one of the most visited (and most atmospheric) temples. The complex originally dates from the late 14th century and the reign of King Ramesuan, although it was largely restored around 1663 by King Prasat Thong. Wat Mahathat was one of the most important temples in Ayutthaya's heyday: the seat of the Supreme Patriarch and with a *prang* that stood around 50m (164ft) high.

From the entrance gate, walk to the right to find a stone Buddha head on the ground trapped in the tangled

roots of a bodhi tree. It is one of the iconic images of Ayutthaya. Around the ruins are numerous headless statues, with just the crossed legs hinting at the meditative positions they once assumed. The Wat Mahathat grounds are large enough to enable you to enjoy serene moments even when accompanied by coach parties.

Wat Ratchaburana

Turn left out of Wat Mahathat and cross the road, where, on the corner, there is another of the city's most significant sites. King Borom Ratchathirat II (Chao Sam Phraya) built **Wat Ratchaburana** (Thanon Maharat; daily 7.30am–6.30pm; charge) in 1424 as a memorial to his elder brothers who killed each other at this spot in an elephant-back duel for the throne. Some murals still exist, while other artworks found during excavations in the late 1950s are now kept in the Chao Sam Phraya Museum. Across Thanon Maharat on the corner of Thanon Naresuan is **Ruean Rojjana**, see ⑪②, if you are hungry at this point.

BACK TO BANGKOK

To leave Ayutthaya, do a U-turn from Wat Ratchaburana and turn left by Ruean Rojjana into Thanon Naresuan. Drive to the end of the road and turn right, then right again just before the bridge. If you go straight ahead, you will come to **Pae Krung Kao Ayudthaya**, see ⑪③, an alternative meal stop 200m/ yds on the left. Follow the road round to go over the bridge and on to Bangkok.

Above from far left: Khun Paen's House; remains of a Buddha image at Wat Ratchaburana; dusk falls on Wat Phra Sri Sanphet.

White Elephants North of Ayutthaya, the Ayutthaya Royal Elephant Kraal is a reconstruction of the site where elephants were trained for warfare, as beasts of burden, and for sale to India. White elephants were regarded as sacred, and any found immediately became the property of the king. Given as gifts by the monarch, they were highly prized, but could also be ruinously expensive – hence the English term 'white elephant' for something less desirable than it originally seems.

PHETCHABURI

Feast on some of Thailand's best-loved desserts, while picking up the flavour of old-fashioned Siam in a small town of 18th-century Ayutthaya-period temples, and the summer palace of King Rama IV.

DISTANCE 132km (84 miles) from Bangkok to Phetchaburi; town tour: 5.5km (3½ miles)
TIME A full day
START Wat Yai Suwannaram
END Phra Nakhon Khiri Park
POINTS TO NOTE
Trains and buses from Bangkok take around three hours (*see left*). If driving, the trip takes about 90 minutes. Take Highway 35 west, then Highway 4 south. On the return journey look out for the road branching left to Samut Songkram to get back onto Highway 35 (heading east). There is no sign for Bangkok, so it is easily missed.

Phetchaburi – usually pronounced Pet-buri – was once a significant port, from where goods were ferried by river and canal to the old Siam capital of Ayutthaya. King Rama IV was one of several kings of the current Chakri dynasty who chose this coastal area as a place to escape the seasonal Bangkok heat.

LOCAL TEMPLES

The town's wats are open to the public daily from 8am–4pm at no charge; four are of particular interest. Start the tour at **Wat Yai Suwannaram ❶** on Phong-suriya Road. Thought to have once been a residence of King Suea, it has many ornately tiled buildings within a low-walled complex, and fine murals that are among the country's oldest. The stucco work is of a style that predates the symmetric Ayutthayan motifs that came to dominate Thai architecture. The old library building on stilts in the middle of the pond illustrates an early method of protecting manuscripts from termites.

Turn right out of the wat and right again onto Phokarong Road, where **Wat Kamphaeng Laeng ❷** sits 800m/yds further down on the right. The sandstone wall of the compound is partly original, as are four Khmer-style *prangs*, one of which contains a Buddha footprint relic. Next, turn right down Phra Song Road for about 1km (²/₃ mile) until you reach the crossroads at Matayawong Road, then turn left. After 800m/yds turn right at the clock tower to find **Wat Ko Keo Sutharam ❸**, 50m/yds on the left. The fading but beautiful murals here, which date from 1734, depict the previous lives of the Buddha.

On leaving, turn left on to Phanit Charoen Road. After 800m/yds turn left at Phra Song Road and follow it to the large white tower of **Wat Mahathat ❹**, which contains many murals and a statue of five integrated Buddhas.

DAY MARKET

Retrace your steps on Phra Song Road and turn left into Phanit Charoen Road, where the **Day Market** ❺ is 150m/yds on the right. Phetchaburi is reputed to have the country's finest palm sugar, so visiting Thais will invariably leave with a souvenir bag of the famous local desserts. Follow suit, and also look out for another local speciality called *khao chae*, a dish of cold rice in chilled, jasmine-infused water, accompanied by titbits like stuffed chillis and fresh fruit.

KING'S RETREAT

Stay on Phanit Charoen Road then turn left after 100m/yds onto Chisa-In Road, which almost immediately crosses the river. Take the next right, then left at Ratchawithi Road, and continue 1.5km (1 mile) to the end, passing the **Krua Thai** café, see ❶①. Directly ahead you can start the ascent to **Phra Nakhon Khiri Historical Park** ❻ (daily 8.30am–4.30pm; charge). If you don't want to climb, turn right, then immediately left at the traffic lights. Then, just after the green overhead signs to Bangkok, go left at the road marked 'cable car'. After 200m/yds a white building marks another entrance to the park and cable-car access (B70, including park entry). There are some places for snacks here, too. Don't take food with you: the hillside is populated by potentially aggressive wild monkeys.

Amid the trees at the top are several temples and a **summer palace** of King Rama IV (1851–68), who was the subject of several books and the film *The King & I*, based on the memoirs of Anna Leonowens. All are regarded in Thailand as disrespectful to the monarchy and are banned.

The Thai, Chinese and European interior of the palace gives a sense of royal life at the time. The building is very modest, and the king's own quarters positively cell-like, perhaps befitting someone who spent many years in a monastery before ascending the throne. There is a great view of the surrounding countryside, and the cool breeze passing through the wooden shutters illustrates why this was such a good spot to spend the summer.

Above from far left: Khmer-style *prang* of Wat Kamphaeng Laeng; tourists trekking up to the summer palace of King Rama IV; rooftops of Wat Yai Suwannaram.

Food and Drink

① KRUA THAI
57 Ratchawithi Road; tel: 0 3242 6941; $
A blue Thai-language sign on the window marks this air-conditioned café, which serves decent rice meals, stir-fries and soups. It is on the left, 150m/yds before Phra Nakhon Khiri Historical Park.

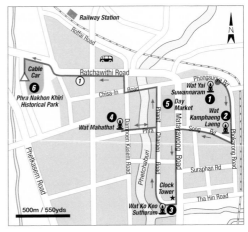

HUA HIN

Despite its modern role as a tourist attraction, this small seaside town retains an air of tranquillity and has been favoured as a summer seat by the royal family since the early 19th century.

There and Back

Buses to Hua Hin run from Bangkok's Southern Bus Terminal (147 Thanon Borom-ratchachonnani; tel: 0 2435 5605). Trains go from Hualamphong Station (1 Thanon Rong Muang; tel: 1690; www.railway.co.th).

Hua Hin's bus and and train stations are both a short walk from the town's night market. The last bus to Bangkok leaves at 9pm, but the last train is at 4pm. Staying the night is the most relaxing option. For accommodation in Hua Hin, *see p.115.*

DISTANCE 195km (121 miles) from Bangkok to Hua Hin; town tour: 15.5km (9⅔ miles)

TIME A full day

START Hua Hin Railway Station

END Hua Hin Night Market

POINTS TO NOTE

If driving, take Highway 35 then Highway 4 (2½–3 hours). The tour assumes you will be driving, but if you come by public transport you can still get around *(see margin, right)*. On the return journey look out for the road branching left to Samut Songkram to get back onto Highway 35 towards Bangkok.

Trains and buses from Bangkok take three to four hours. Be sure to check return times *(see margin, left)*.

Prachuap Kiri Khan is Thailand's narrowest province and its coast is fringed with mountains and lovely quiet beaches, the most popular of which is the 5km (3-mile) long sandy beach at Hua Hin.

The town gained royal favour when King Rama VI constructed a seafront summer palace here in 1922. **Phra Ratchawang Klai Kangwon** (Far From Worries Palace) led to an influx of high society, and so began the sleepy fishing village's transformation into a tourist hotspot. The current royal family still visit here.

RAILWAY STATION

Built in 1923, **Hua Hin Railway Station ❶** is the town's second-most famous building. Although the lane in which it sits is now filled with traffic, the dainty teak structure still possesses much of its original charm. Golf is a booming sport in Thailand, and across the single-rail track (one of Thailand's first rail lines, linking the town with Bangkok) is the **Royal Hua Hin Golf Course** (Damnern Kasem Road; tel: 0 3251 2475; daily 6am–6pm; charge), built in 1924, where it all began.

Leave the station, go down Damnern Kasem Road and turn right at the traffic lights into Phetchakasem Road.

Food and Drink 🍴

① CHAO LAY
15 Naresdamri Road; tel: 0 3251 3436; $$
One of the most popular of several restaurants on stilts over the sea. All kinds of fresh seafood are served grilled, deep-fried or steamed.

② BRASSERIE DE PARIS
3 Naresdamri Road; tel: 08 1826 6814; $$$
Sit upstairs at this wooden pier restaurant for views of fishing boats bobbing on the waves. It has delicious freshly caught seafood served French-style, such as rock lobster *au beurre blanc.*

After 3km (2 miles) bear left beside the flyover, following signs to Khao Takiab. On the bend is the **Chiva-Som** guests-only health resort, where the likes of supermodel Kate Moss come to be pampered.

KHAO TAKIAB

After 2.5km (1½ miles) go left at the major fork, follow the road as it bends left and head uphill to the summit of **Khao Takiab** ❷ (Chopstick Hill). Here there are souvenir stalls, cafés and a temple where a tree shades Buddha images and a troupe of monkeys feed on bananas proffered by tourists. A narrow road circling the summit has views of the Gulf of Thailand, as does **La Mer** restaurant (tel: 0 3253 6205), which serves Thai food.

COLONIAL HOTEL

Driving back to town, turn right at the first traffic lights into Damnern Kasem Road. At the bottom of the slope go right and then left into the **Sofitel Centara Hua Hin** ❸, Thailand's first resort accommodation when it was built as the Railway Hotel in 1923. The beautifully preserved colonial setting ensures it is a popular film location, most famously used in *The Killing Fields* (1984). Park here, and have afternoon tea in **The Museum**, an open-sided pavilion that benefits from gentle breezes and views of the gardens and the sea beyond. Old artefacts and photos are displayed around the room.

SHOPPING

Afterwards, wander onto the beach and turn left. After 50m/yds go left beside the pony hire, continue for 100m/yds and turn right into **Naresdamri Road** ❹, the tourist shopping street, with enticements such as Thai massage, Indian tailors, bars and restaurants.

After 200m/yds you come to **Chao Lay**, see ⑪①, and beyond that **Brasserie de Paris**, see ⑪②. Opposite Chao Lay is Hua Hin Soi 57; turn left here and cross two main roads (Naeb Khaehat and Phetchakasem) into Decha Nuchit Road, where **Hua Hin Night Market** ❺ is open from 5–11pm daily. It is a great place to sample street food and stock up on souvenirs such as Thai silks, crafts and jewellery.

Above from far left:
boats on the beach; luxury Hilton Hua Hin at dusk.

Notes and Boats
The three-day Hua Hin Jazz Festival features local and international bands on the beach every June, while sailors come from far and wide for the Hua Hin Regatta in July or August.

On the Move
If you cut out Chiva-Som and Khao Takiab, this tour is achievable on foot. Otherwise, there are cars (B1,300/day) and motorbikes (B200/day) to rent opposite the entrance to the Sofitel Centara. Parking is available for a small fee in the grounds of Wat Hua Hin, on Phetcha-kasem Road, on the left just after the clock tower coming from Bangkok.

PATTAYA

After a relaxing afternoon amid tropical gardens and a carved wooden temple overlooking the waves, change pace and head for Pattaya's pulsating nightlife, full of bars and bands and the sequinned excess of ladyboy cabaret.

DISTANCE 140km (87 miles) to Pattaya; town tour via Nong Nooch: 55km (33.5 miles)

TIME A full day

START The Sanctuary of Truth

END Beach Road

POINTS TO NOTE

The journey is best done by car (2 hours). From Bangkok take Highway 7 (heading east then south), which joins Sukhumvit Road at Pattaya. Otherwise, catch a bus (every 30 minutes, 5am–10pm from Bangkok's Eastern Bus Terminal) and hail a *songthaew* (pick-up truck) to get around. Stay overnight to make the most of the nightlife; for accommodation options, *see p.115*.

Annual Happenings

Events to look out for in the annual calendar include the three-day Pattaya Music Festival, with local and foreign acts, in March, the Top of the Gulf Regatta in May and the Pattaya Marathon in July. The nearby town of Chonburi has buffalo racing in October.

Outdoor Pursuits

Sporting activities include golf at Siam Country Club (Soi Siam Country Club; tel: 0 3890 9700; www.siamcountryclub.com); diving with Aquanauts Dive Centre (437/17 Pattaya Beach Road, Soi 6; tel: 0 3836 1724; www.aquanautsdive.com); riding at Horseshoe Point (100 Moo 9, Tambon Phong; tel: 0 3873 5050; www.horseshoepoint.com); skydiving at Pattaya Airpark (108/1 Moo 9, Hui Yai; tel: 08 6374 1718; www.pattayaairpark.com) or zip lining through the jungle on The Flight of the Gibbon (Khao Kheow Open Zoo; tel: 08 9970 5511; www.treetopasia.com).

Pattaya may be notorious for its sex trade – a legacy of US soldiers on leave during the Vietnam War – but less raunchy attractions also entice a steady flow of family visitors.

With a 10am start from Bangkok you will arrive in time for a seafront lunch. Entering Pattaya from Highway 7, turn right, then after 500m/yds go left into Naklua Road. After 300m/yds turn right into Naklua Soi 4, where you can lunch at **Mumaroi**, see ①①, on the left.

THE SANCTUARY OF TRUTH

Turn right from the restaurant and rejoin Naklua Road, driving straight ahead into the old fishing village of Naklua. Look out for the spirit tree where fishermen leave offerings in the hope of safety and a good catch. After 3km (2 miles) turn right into Naklua Soi 12. Bearing left where the road forks, you will come to the first sight on this tour, the **Sanctuary of Truth** ❶ (tel: 0 3836 7229; www.sanctuaryoftruth. com; daily 8am–6pm; charge). This extraordinary building appears like a fairy-tale castle on the water's edge. Over 100m (328ft) high, it is made entirely of hardwoods, intricately carved with figures of gods and spirits. It is a

work in progress; you can watch the carpenters and even take up tools yourself.

NONG NOOCH

Leave the sanctuary, turn right at Naklua Road, and follow the road until you reach a roundabout. You could head straight across to reach Beach Road. Alternatively, to visit the tropical gardens at Nong Nooch, turn left into North Pattaya Road and right at the top into Sukhumvit Road. After 22.5km (14 miles) turn left to **Nong Nooch ❷** (163 Sukhumvit Road, Sattaheep; tel: 0 3870 9358; www.nongnoochtropicalgarden. com; daily 8am–6pm; charge). Here you can see gibbons and tigers, as well as flamingos and hornbills. There is also Thai boxing and elephant rides.

TIFFANY'S CABARET

From Nong Nooch, return on the route to Pattaya, turning left at Central Pattaya Road, then right at the crossroads into Pattaya 2nd Road. After 1km (⅔

mile), on the left beside Soi Srinakorn is **Tiffany's ❸** (464 Moo 9, Pattaya 2nd Road; tel: 0 3842 1700; www.tiffany-show.co.th; shows at 6pm, 7.30pm and 9pm; charge), which hosts Thailand's famous ladyboy *(katoey)* shows.

BEACH ROAD

Turn left from Tiffany's, then left again at the roundabout into **Beach Road ❹**. Park somewhere around Soi 13. The roads are awash with market stalls, shopping malls, go-go bars, Brit pubs and cocktail bars. The extension of Beach Road is **Walking Street**, where you will find **King Seafood**, see ⑪②.

Above from far left:
Sanctuary of Truth; seafront; ladyboy show.

Night Market
Pattaya has its own mini Chatuchak at Thepprasit Market (Fri–Sun 5–11pm), which runs close to the junction of Thepprasit and Sukhumvit roads. It sells the usual eclectic mass of knock-off watches, bags, T-shirts and interior decorations, and is packed with Thai food stalls.

Food and Drink

① MUMAROI
83/4 Moo 2, Naklua Soi 4; tel: 0 3822 3252; $–$$
Order fantastic deep-fried sea bass, curried crab and spicy seafood salad to enjoy along with the sea view.

② KING SEAFOOD
94 Walking Street; tel: 0 3842 9459; $$
Choose your lobster, crab, shrimp and fish either from the tanks or the display on ice at this restaurant built on stilts above the lapping waves.

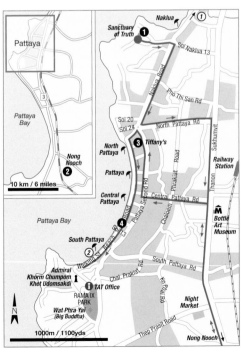

DIRECTORY

A user-friendly alphabetical listing of practical information, plus hand-picked hotels and restaurants, clearly organised by area, to suit all budgets and tastes. Select nightlife listings are also included here.

A

ADDRESSES

Given the size of the city and its many twisting alleyways, finding your way around Bangkok can be a bit confusing. Main roads often have smaller streets – called *sois* – leading off them, each having the main road's name followed by a number. For example, Thanon Sukhumvit (Sukhumvit Road) has side streets called Sukhumvit Soi 1, Sukhumvit Soi 3, etc., running in sequence, with odd and even numbers found on opposite sides of the road. *Sois* may be subdivided using a slash after the number followed by another number. The same system is used for shop and house addresses, a slash separating the block or building number from the shop. So an address might read 36/1 Sukhumvit 33/1.

Confusingly, the roads can have as many as four names, based on local usage, often reflecting the most important building in each. Street names are usually written in Thai and English *(see margin, right)*, and most hotels provide business cards with the address written in Thai, to show taxi drivers. In tourist areas street names are often given in English, for example, Naklua Road.

B

BUDGETING

Despite spiralling prices, by Western standards Bangkok is a bargain. Budget accommodation can be as cheap as B200 a night, with a delicious street-side meal and beer around B120. Five-star hotels cost from B6,000, while a three-course meal may be had for B1,000 without drinks (although wine is expensive, and one bottle will at least double that price). Refreshments in bars start around B60, and even in posh clubs they may be as little as B200. Bus fares cost B7–22, a Skytrain or metro ride B16–40 and taxi meters start at B35 *(also see p.107)*. If you live frugally, you can get by on B500 a day.

BUSINESS HOURS

Government offices operate Mon–Fri 8.30am–4.30pm, most businesses Mon–Fri 8am–5.30pm (some also Sat 8.30am–noon) and banks Mon–Fri 9.30am–3.30pm. Money-changing kiosks are open daily until 8pm.

Shops generally open 10am–8pm, with some variations depending on location and the type of business. Department stores open daily 10.30am–9pm or 10pm.

Small open-air coffee shops and traditional Thai restaurants open at 7am and close at 8.30pm, though some stay open past midnight. Modern indoor restaurants generally close by 10pm. Some hotel coffee shops stay open 24 hours, and the city has several outdoor restaurants that are open as late as 4am for after-hours suppers. Clubs and bars are subject to loosely applied licensing laws and may close anywhere between midnight and 5am, depending on location and political and policing climate.

C

CHILDREN

Travelling with children is not especially difficult in Thailand, although Bangkok pavements are often in disrepair and invariably obstructed by something or someone. When travelling with babies, leave the buggy at home, and bring back- or chest-mounted baby carriers. Many department stores and malls have play areas and baby-changing facilities, and some up-market hotels have baby-sitting services. The tropical heat is intense, so sunblock and sunhats are important, while keeping hands clean helps to ward off stomach bugs.

CLIMATE

There are three seasons in Bangkok: hot (March–mid-June): 27–35°C (80–95°F); rainy (June–October): 24–32°C (75–90°F); cool (November–February): 18–32°C (65–90°F), and with less humidity.

CLOTHING

Clothes should be light, loose and preferably made of natural fibres, which breathe better. Shorts are fine to wear in most situations, although not in temples, where legs and shoulders should be covered. A shirt and tie are expected for business appointments. A hat will offer protection from the fierce sun, and it is obviously wise to carry an umbrella during the rainy season.

CRIME AND SAFETY

Although Bangkok, like all cities, has an underbelly of violent crime, tourists rarely encounter it, and the streets are generally very safe. The biggest risk to travellers is from scams and con artists *(see p.19)*. If you do run into trouble, contact the Tourist Police: Tourist Service Centre, TAT headquarters, 4 Thanon Ratchadamnoen Nok; tel: 0 2281 5051; hotline: 1155. Tourist police booths can be found in tourist areas, including Lumphini Park (near the intersection of Rama IV and Silom) and Patpong (at the Surawong intersection). Most tourist police speak some English.

CUSTOMS

The Thai government prohibits the import or export of drugs, dangerous chemicals, pornography, firearms, ammunition and goods that display the Thai flag. The maximum penalty for smuggling hard drugs is death.

Tourists have a duty-free allowance of 200 cigarettes and 1 litre of wine or spirits. Foreign currency over US$20,000 entering or leaving the country should be declared. Thai currency leaving the country is limited to B50,000.

VAT refunds are available on completion of necessary paperwork at the airport. Buddha images, antiques and art objects must have a Department of Fine Arts permit, which can be arranged by the vendor (or tel: 0 2224 1333). Pre-18th-century items must not be exported. Check www.customs-clinic.org, or call the hotline: 1164.

Above from far left: bumper-car driving; taking some time out in Siam Square; Suvarnabhumi Airport handles all international flights.

Street Names
Not only do some streets often have several different names, but with no standard transliterated English spellings for the Thai language, it is common to find a street or area spelt with several variants and broken or joined syllables.

D

DISABLED TRAVELLERS

Bangkok falls short on accommo-
dating people with disabilities. The
uneven pavements are studded with
obstructions, and few buildings have
wheelchair ramps. Traffic is relentless,
and drivers are generally unsympa-
thetic to pedestrians. However, there
have been signs of improvement in
recent years. Only a few Skytrain stations have lifts, but the metro has them
at every station, and more expensive
hotels and shopping malls often have
disabled access and modified toilets.
Taxi drivers, if arranged beforehand, can
be quite cooperative. However, it may be
preferable to travel with a companion.

E

ELECTRICITY

Electrical outlets are rated at 220 volts,
50 cycles and accept flat- or round-
pronged plugs. Adaptors are cheap to
buy at department or hardware stores.

EMBASSIES

Australia: 37 Thanon Sathorn Tai; tel:
0 2344 6300. Visas: Mon–Fri 8.30am–
3pm from Thai CC Tower, 889
Thanon Sathorn Tai; tel: 0 2672 3476.
Canada: 15/F Abdulrahim Place, Thanon Rama IV; tel: 0 2636 0540; 2254
2530. Visas: Mon–Thur 7.30am–10am.
New Zealand: M Thai Tower, 14/F
All Seasons Place, 87 Thanon Withayu; tel: 0 2254 2530. Visas: Mon–Fri
9am–noon, 1pm–2.30pm.
United Kingdom: 14 Thanon Withayu; tel: 0 2305 8333. Visas: Mon–Fri
8.30am–3.30pm from Fl2; Regent
House, 183 Thanon Ratchadamri;
tel: 0 2800 8050.
United States: 120–2 Thanon Withayu; tel: 0 2205 4000. Visas: Mon–Fri
7am–4pm, by appointment only at 95
Thanon Withayu.

EMERGENCIES

Police: 191.
Tourist Police: emergency hotline tel:
1155; or 0 2281 5051, or 0 2664 0222.

ETIQUETTE

Thais are remarkably tolerant, but
there are a few things that upset them:

Buddhism: It is impolite to point your
feet at Buddha images or to have bare
legs or shoulders when visiting temples.
Monks have taken vows of celibacy,
and women should avoid physical contact with them, including passing items
directly to them. Instead, place the
object somewhere to be picked up.

Head and feet: Thais believe the head
and feet to be the highest and lowest
parts of the body, spiritually as well as
physically. It is therefore seen as
insulting to touch another person's
head, to move items with your feet, or
to step over another person.
Intimacy: Public shows of affection
rarely extend beyond holding hands.

Terms of address: Thais are addressed by their first names, usually preceded by the word Khun, the equivalent of Mr or Ms. For example, Silpachai Krishnamra would be addressed as Khun Silpachai.

Thai greetings: The common greeting and farewell in Thailand is *Sawasdee*, (followed by *khrap* when spoken by men and *kha* by women). In more formal settings this is accompanied by a *wai* – raising the hands in a prayer-like gesture, the fingertips touching the nose, and bowing the head slightly. In business meetings the *wai* is often followed by a handshake. Foreigners are not expected to *wai*.

The Royal Family: Thais have a great reverence for the monarchy, and disapprove of any disrespect directed towards members of the royal family. Thailand also has lese-majesty laws that, although usually invoked to settle business or political rivalries, may result in jail terms for people convicted of defaming, insulting or threatening royalty. Standing for the national anthem is expected in cinemas regardless of your nationality.

G

GAY AND LESBIAN

The gay nightlife scene is thriving and the city hosts an on-off Bangkok Gay Pride Festival (www.bangkokpride.org) in November. Find updates on the useful resource site www.utopia-asia.com or at Purple Dragon, a travel agency that caters exclusively for gay travellers (Tarntawan Place Hotel, 119/5-10 Thanon Surawong; tel: 0 2634 3186; www.purpledrag.com).

H

HEALTH

Visitors entering Thailand are not required to show evidence of vaccinations, but do check that tetanus boosters are up-to-date. Inoculations for cholera and hepatitis A and B are a good idea. When in border areas with Cambodia, Laos and Myanmar apply mosquito repellent on exposed skin at all times; ideally, cover up to protect against malaria and dengue fever.

It is important to drink plenty of water and use sunblock. Tap water in Bangkok has been certified drinkable, but bottled water is still safer and is easily available. Within Bangkok ice is clean and presents no health problems.

Hospitals and dental clinics: The standard of doctors, equipment and medical care at the following hospitals is excellent. All have English-speaking staff and additional specialised clinics, including dental facilities.

Bangkok Christian Hospital: 124 Thanon Silom; tel: 0 2233 6981–9; www.bkkchristianhosp.th.com.

BNH Hospital: 9/1 Thanon Convent, Silom; tel: 0 2686 2700; www.bnhhospital.com.

Bumrungrad Hospital: 33 Sukhumvit Soi 3, tel: 0 2667 1000; www.bumrungrad.com.

Above from far left: Thai *lakhon* dancers in traditional dress; it is impolite to point your feet at Bhuddha images; making a request at Erawan Shrine.

Hotlines
Where there is an option, it is usually better to call a hotline number. You will get directly to someone who is designated to deal with queries, rather than going the through the switchboard and several different people.

Internet
Wi-fi zones are a fast-growing phenomenon, found at the airport, in some hotels and at some branches of Starbucks. Major hotel internet services usually include in-room; even smaller hotels sometimes have internet access available. Public internet cafés mainly have reasonable speed broadband for around B30 per hour. There are many located around Khao San Road. Otherwise, your hotel concierge should know the nearest available.

Left Luggage
There are two left luggage facilities at Suvarnabhumi Airport on the second and fourth floors. The fee is B100 per piece per day. Hotels and guesthouses offer a left-luggage service, usually for a small daily fee.

Medical clinics: For minor problems, the British Dispensary, 109 Thanon Sukhumvit (between *sois* 3 and 5), tel: 0 2252 8056, has British doctors on its staff. Major hotels have an on-site clinic or a doctor on call.

Pharmacies: There are many branches of Boots and Watson's pharmacies in central Bangkok, including in shopping malls. Many antibiotics and other drugs are available without a prescription. Always check the expiry date.

L

LANGUAGE

English is widely used in hotels and shops, but it is always appreciated when visitors try to use some Thai.

Bangkokians speak the Central dialect, one of four major dialects in the country. Thai has its own script, with 44 consonants and 32 vowels, and also has five tones: low, middle, high, falling and rising. The meaning of a word changes with the tone; an oft-used example is 'new wood doesn't burn', which in Thai is *'mai mai mai mai'*, each word having a different tone and thus a different meaning.

Transliteration of Thai into the Roman alphabet is difficult, as there are only a few one-to-one phonological correspondences. The transliterations we use include:

k	like the 'k' in 'skin'
kh	like the 'k' in 'kite'
p	like the 'p' in 'stopper' (not the

'p' in 'pat')
ph	like the 'p' in 'pat' (never as the 'ph' in 'phone')
t	like the 't' in 'forty' (not the 't' in 'top')
th	like the 't' in 'top'
ng	like the 'ng' in 'hang', but used as an initial consonant

To be polite, men should end each sentence with the syllable *khrap*. Women should end each sentence with *kha*.

Some useful basic words of vocabulary are included on the pull-out map that accompanies this book.

LOST PROPERTY

Report lost property as soon as possible to the Tourist Police (hotline: 1155; *see also p.99*) to get an insurance statement.
Airport: tel: 0 2132 1888.
Public transit: BMTA city bus service, tel: 0 2246 0973; BTS Skytrain, tel: 0 2617 6000; MRTA subway, tel: 0 2624 6200, Hualamphong Railway Station, hotline: 1690.
Taxis: taxi hotline (tel: 1644); or JS100 Radio 100FM hotline (tel: 1137), to which taxi drivers often respond.

M

MAPS

Basic maps of Bangkok are available free at the Tourism Authority of Thailand (TAT) offices *(see p.105)* and at big hotels. More detailed ones can be found in bookshops. The Insight

Fleximap and Nelles Map of Bangkok are both good. The colourful hand-drawn Nancy Chandler's Map of Bangkok is good on local knowledge and has useful margin tips to cultural attractions, markets, shops, etc.

MEDIA

Newspapers and magazines: the *Bangkok Post* and *The Nation* are both English-language daily newspapers. The free weekly magazine, *BK*, found in several restaurants, and cafés such as Starbucks, keeps up with events around town.

Radio: English-language stations come and go frequently. At the time of writing, options include Wave FM (88FM) and www.radiobangkok.net.

Television: True Visions network has film, sport, news and entertainment channels such as HBO, ESPN, BBC World News and MTV Thailand.

MONEY

ATMs: These are available at banks, malls, major train and bus stations, and airports. Many accept credit cards and MasterCard and Visa debit cards.
Changing money: Banking hours are Mon–Fri 9.30am–3.30pm, but most banks maintain money-changing kiosks in tourist areas. Better hotels will change money, but generally at poor rates.

Credit cards: American Express, Diner's Club, MasterCard, JCB and

Visa are widely accepted. Credit cards can be used to draw cash at most banks. If you lose your credit card, call:
American Express: tel: 0 2273 5222.
Diner's Club: tel: 0 2238 3660.
Visa: tel: 001 800 441 3485.
MasterCard: tel: 001 800 11-887 0663.
Credit card fraud is a major problem in Thailand. Do not leave your credit card in safe-deposit boxes. When making a purchase, ensure you get the carbon copies and dispose of them.

Local currency: The baht is the principal Thai monetary unit, with banknote denominations of 1,000, 500, 100, 50 and 20. There are 10, 5, 2 and 1 baht, plus 50- (half baht/50 satang) and 25-satang coins.

Taxes: Thailand has a Value Added Tax (VAT) of 7 percent. This is added to most goods and services (but not goods sold by street vendors and markets). You can get the VAT refunded *(see p.99)* if your total purchases come to B5,000-worth of goods or more.

Major hotels add VAT and 10 per-cent service charge to the room rate, as do mid- to high-priced restaurants.

Tipping: Tipping is not a custom in Thailand, although it is becoming more common in upper-end establish-ments. However, people generally leave any loose change left over from their bill, both in food shops and taxis.

Traveller's cheques: These can be cashed at all exchange kiosks and banks, at a charge of B25 each.

Above from far left: Suvarnabhumi Airport offers a left-luggage service; baht banknote with the image of King Rama IX.

Be Prepared
If you plan on using your credit card a lot, it may be worth taking an alternative one as a backup in case you run into problems through fraud or theft.

P

POSTAL SERVICES

The Thai postal service is pretty reliable, though registering or sending items by EMS can improve the odds for domestic mail. Courier services are preferable for valuable parcels or bulky documents sent overseas.

The General Post Office is located between Charoen Krung *sois* 32 and 34 (tel: 0 2233 1050; Mon–Fri 8am–8pm, Sat–Sun and public holidays 8am–1pm). Post offices elsewhere in Bangkok usually open Mon–Fri 8am–4pm. The GPO and many larger offices sell packing boxes and materials.

Courier services:

DHL: tel: 0 2631 2621; www.dhl.co.th.
Fedex: tel: 0 2229 8800, or hotline: 1782; www.fedex.com/th.
UPS: tel: 0 2762 3300; www.ups.com/th.

PUBLIC HOLIDAYS

1 Jan: New Year's Day
Late Feb/Mar: (full moon) Magha Puja. Note: Chinese New Year is not an official holiday, but many businesses close for several days.
6 Apr: Chakri Day
13–15 Apr: Songkran
1 May: Labour Day
5 May: Coronation Day
Early May: Royal Ploughing Ceremony (officials only)
Late May/June: (full moon) Visakha Puja
Late July/Aug: (full moon) Asanha

Puja and Khao Pansa
12 Aug: Queen's Birthday (Mothers' Day)
23 Oct: King Chulalongkorn Day
5 Dec: King's Birthday (Fathers' Day)
10 Dec: Constitution Day

R

RELIGION

Although it is predominantly Buddhist, Thailand has historically been tolerant of other religions. Buddhist temples are plentiful and there are several mosques, a major Hindu temple and a handful of Christian churches and synagogues.

Anglican and Episcopalian: Christ Church Bangkok, 11 Convent Road; tel: 0 2234 3634. Sunday services at 7.30am, 10am and 5pm.
Catholic: Holy Redeemer Church, 123/19 Soi Ruam Rudi, Thanon Withayu; tel: 0 2256 6305. Sunday mass at 8.30am, 9.45am, 11am and 5.30pm.
Jewish: Even Chen Synagogue, Chao Phraya Office Tower, Shangri-La Hotel, Charoen Krung Soi 42/1; tel: 0 2236 7777. Services daily at 9am.
Muslim: Assalafiyah Mosque, 2827 Thanon Charoen Krung; tel: 0 2688 1481. Service times vary.

T

TELEPHONES

International calls: The country code for Thailand is 66. When calling Thailand from overseas, dial your local

Photography
Camera shops and photo development outlets are commonly found in the tourist areas, and most offer digital transfers onto CD and hard copy photos from digital. Prints are available at B3–4 each, with bigger enlargements a real bargain.

international access code, followed by 66 and the 8-digit number (without the preceding 0). To make an international call from Thailand, dial 001 or 009 before the country and area codes, followed by the telephone number. For international call assistance, dial 100.

Prepaid phone cards (Thaicard) for international calls are available at post offices and shops with the Thaicard sign.

Local calls: Area codes in Thailand are merged with phone numbers. The prefix 0 must be dialled for all calls made within Thailand, even when calling local numbers in Bangkok. Dial 0 first, followed by the 8-digit number. For local directory assistance, dial 1133.

Any number that begins with 08 is a local mobile number.

Public telephones: These accept B1, B5 and B10 coins. Phonecards for local calls (B50, B100, B200 and B400) are available at convenience shops: there are several available, some are cheaper, particularly for international calls. Call the phone company hotlines for options (CAT, tel: 1322; TOT, tel: 1100).

and kiosks within Thailand that offer maps and other promotional materials, as well as advice on things to do and places to see. The website www.tourism thailand.org has plenty of information. **TAT Call Centre**: tel: 1672; daily 8am–8pm.

TAT Main Office: 1600 Thanon New Phetchaburi, Makkasan, Bangkok 10400; tel: 0 2250 5500; daily 8.30am–4.30pm.

TAT Tourist Information Counters: Arrivals Hall, Suvarnabhumi Airport; tel: 0 2504 2701; daily 8am–10pm.

4 Thanon Ratchadamnoen Nok; tel: 0 2282 9774; daily 8.30am–4.30pm.

Overseas Offices
Australia and New Zealand: Suite 2002, Level 20, 56 Pitt Street, Sydney, NSW 2000; tel: +61 2 9247 7549.
UK: 3rd Floor, Brook House, 98–9 Jermyn Street, London SW1 6EE; tel: +44 20 7925 2511.
US: 61 Broadway, Suite 2810, New York, NY 10006; tel: +1 212 432 0433; and 611 North Larchmont Boulevard, 1st Floor, Los Angeles, CA 90004; tel: +1 323 461 9814.

TIME DIFFERENCE

Thailand is 7 hours ahead of GMT. Since it gets dark between 6–7pm uniformly throughout the year, Thailand does not observe daylight saving time.

TOURIST INFORMATION

The Tourism Authority of Thailand (TAT) has offices in several countries

TRANSPORT

Getting There

By air: Bangkok's Suvarnabhumi Airport (tel: 0 2132 1888; www.airportthai.co.th) is located about 30km (19 miles) east of Bangkok. The airport handles all international flights to Bangkok as well as many domestic connections.

A small number of Thai Airways domestic flights and all domestic

flights operated by Nok Air, Solar Air and Orient Thai use Don Mueang Airport (tel: 0 2535 1111; www.airportthai.co.th). Don Mueang is about 30km (19 miles) north of the city centre.

It takes around 45 minutes, depending on traffic, to get to or from either airport by taxi. The Suvarnabhumi Airport Rail Link connects that airport with the city and there are also airport shuttles or BMTA public buses from both airports, plus train connections from Don Mueang; check the website for details.

By rail: The State Railway of Thailand (tel: 0 2222 0175, hotline: 1690; www.railway.co.th) operates trains that are generally clean, cheap and reliable. There are three entry points by rail into Thailand. Two are from Malaysia, the more popular of which is the daily train that leaves Butterworth near Penang at 1.15pm for Hat Yai (south Thailand) and arrives in Bangkok's Hualamphong Station at 10.50am the next morning. Trains leave Hualamphong daily at 2.45pm for Malaysia. There is also a short line from Nong Khai, in northeast Thailand, to 3km (2 miles) across the Laos border. This will eventually extend to Vientiane.

By road: Malaysia provides the main road access into Thailand, with crossings near Betong and Sungai Kolok. From Laos you can cross the Mekong River from Vientiane into Nong Khai, or from Savannakhet to Mukhadan, by using one of the 'Friendship Bridges'. From Cambodia the most commonly used border crossing is from Poipet. Another option is to go overland from Kompong Cham in Cambodia, crossing over to Hat Lek in Thailand.

Getting Around

Metro: Bangkok's underground MRT stations stretch between Bang Sue, in the northern suburbs, and the city's main railway station, Hualamphong, at the edge of Chinatown. Three stations – Silom, Sukhumvit and Chatuchak Park – link to the BTS network. The air-conditioned trains operate from 6am to midnight (every 2–4 minutes peak, 4–6 minutes off-peak). Fares start at B16, increasing B2–3 every station, with a maximum fare of B41.

Buy coin-sized plastic tokens at kiosks or self-service ticket machines. Passes are also available for unlimited journeys: 1-day (B120), 3-day (B230), plus a stored-value adult card (B200, which includes a B50 deposit).

Customer relations centre: tel: 0 2624 5200; www.bangkokmetro.co.th.

Skytrain: The Bangkok Transit System (BTS) elevated train service, also known as the Skytrain, is the perfect way to beat the traffic. It has two routes: Sukhumvit Line and Silom Line, which intersect at Siam Station. Trains operate from 6am to midnight (every 3 minutes peak, 5 minutes off-peak). Single-trip fares are B15–B40 according to distance. It is useful to buy the 1-day pass (B120; unlimited journeys) or the 30-day adult pass,

Above from far left: Hualamphong railway station; downtown traffic; tuk tuks waiting for passengers.

which comes in three bands, starting at B345, plus B30 administration fee, for 15 journeys. BTS Tourist Information Centres (tel: 0 2617 7340; hotline: 0 2617 6000; www.bts.co.th) are found on the concourse levels of Siam, Phaya Thai and Saphan Taksin stations (daily 8am–8pm).

Taxi: Metered air-conditioned taxis are inexpensive, and comfortably seat 3–4 people. It is best to hail them on the streets; those parked outside hotels usually hustle for a no-meter fare.

The fare is B35 for the first kilometre, then B5–8.50 per kilometre, depending on distance travelled. If stuck in traffic, a small per-minute surcharge kicks in. If your journey crosses town, ask the driver to take the expressway. The toll fare of B25–45 is given to the driver at the payment booth, not at the end of the trip.

Before starting, check that the meter has been reset and turned on. Fares can be negotiated for longer distances outside Bangkok: for instance, to Pattaya (B1,200), Koh Samet (B1,500) or Hua Hin (B1,500–2,000). Drivers often don't speak much English, but should know the locations of major hotels. It is a good idea to have a destination written in Thai.

The following taxi companies will take bookings, for a B20 surcharge:
Siam Taxi: hotline: 1661.
Taxi Thai: tel: 0 2460 0222.

Motorcycle taxi: Stands for motorcycle taxis are noticeable by their drivers – a gathering of men in fluorescent numbered vests found at the mouth of many *sois*, at busy intersections, buildings and markets. Hire only a driver who provides a passenger helmet, and negotiate fares beforehand. Motorcycle taxis are a great way to beat the traffic and economical for short journeys like the length of a street, which will cost B10–20. A B80–100 ride should get you a half-hour trip across most parts of the downtown area. During rush hour (7–9am and 4–6pm), prices are higher. If the driver is going too fast, ask him to slow down: *cha-cha*.

Tuk tuk: Few drivers of these brightly coloured three-wheeled taxis speak English, so best to have your destination written in Thai. Negotiate the fare before you set off. Expect to pay B30–50 for short journeys of a few blocks or 15 minutes, and B50–100 for longer journeys. B100 should get you a half-hour trip across most parts of the downtown area. Although they can be a fun experience, tuk tuk fares are rarely lower than metered taxis, and you ride in the midst of all the traffic fumes.

Bus: Buses are very cheap, but with little English spoken by staff or displayed on signage, finding the right bus can be frustrating. Municipal and private operators all come under the charge of the Bangkok Mass Transit Authority (BMTA) (tel: 0 2246 0973; www.bmta.co.th). Free maps found at the airport and tourist centres often have bus routes marked.

Station Names
Skytrain station names often differ from the street sign spelling, so Chidlom district becomes Chit Lom Station, Thanon Asoke becomes Asok Station, and Soi Thonglor becomes Thong Lo.

Weights and Measurements
Thailand uses the metric system, except for the traditional system of land measurement (1 rai = 1,600 sq m) and gold (1 baht = 15.2g).

Boat: The Chao Phraya Express Boat Company (tel: 0 2623 6143; www.chaophrayaboat.co.th) runs several services between Nonthaburi Pier in the north to Ratburana in the south. Boats run every 15 minutes from 6am to 9pm, and stop at different piers according to the coloured flag on top of the boat. Yellow and green flags are fastest, but stop at only 12 piers, while orange flags are slowest but stop at every pier. On Saturday and Sunday there are only orange-flag services. Tickets cost B14–34 and are purchased from the conductor on board or at some pier counters.

The company also runs charters and the Chao Phraya Tourist Boat, which operates daily from 9.30am to 3pm, for B120 a ticket (which you can also use after 3.30pm on regular express boats). A useful commentary is provided on board, along with a small guidebook and a bottle of water. The route begins at the Tha Sathorn (Sathom Pier) and travels upriver to the Tha Phra Athit, with 10 stops in between. Boats leave every 30 minutes, and you can get off at any pier and pick up another boat later on this hop-on-and-off service.

There are also cross-river ferries close to the piers that service the Chao Phraya River Express Boats. Costing B2.5 per journey, they operate from 5am to 10pm, or later.

Longtail boat taxis ply the river and narrow inner canals, carrying passengers from the centre of town to the outskirts. Many piers are located near road bridges. Tell the conductor your destination, as boats do not stop otherwise. Tickets cost B5–10, depending on distance, with services operating roughly every 10 minutes until 6–7pm. Visitors will probably only need the main downtown canal, Khlong Saen Saep, which travels from Tha Saphan Phanfah, near Wat Saket, into the heart of the downtown area and on to Bang Kapi. It can be a useful route to Jim Thompson's House, Siam Centre and the Thanon Ploenchit malls.

If you wish to explore the canals of Thonburi or Nonthaburi, private long-tail boats can be hired from most of the river's main piers. A 90-minute to two-hour tour will take you into the quieter canal communities. Enquire beforehand which route the boat will take and what will be seen along the way, and negotiate rates (B700–800 for an hour, B1,000 and over for two hours). The price is for the entire boat, which may seat up to 16 people. On the trip, ask to pull up and get out if anything interests you.

Car rental: Thailand has a good road system, with signs in both Thai and English, and driving is largely comfortable, although with a few caveats. Tailgating and hazardous overtaking are common, lane discipline is erratic, and right of way is often determined by size. Motorcycles are numerous, so the use of mirrors needs to be constant. If you are not confident, car or van rental with a driver is available.

An international driver's licence is required to drive yourself. Car rental starts around B800 a day, including

insurance, but it is worth phoning around, as prices vary greatly.

Avis: 2/12 Thanon Withayu; tel: 0 2255 5300-4; and Bangkok International Airport Building 2; tel: 0 84 700 8157-9; www.avisthailand.com.

Hertz: Soi 71, Thanon Sukhumvit; tel: 0 2266 4666; www.hertz.com.

Sathorn Car Rent: 6/8-9 Thanon Sathorn; tel: 0 2633 8888.

V

VISAS AND PASSPORTS

Travellers should check visa regulations at a Thai embassy or consulate before starting their trip, as visa rules vary for different nationalities. For an updated list, check the Thai Ministry of Foreign Affairs website at www. mfa.go.th.

All foreign nationals entering Thailand must have valid passports with at least six months before the expiry date. Nationals from most countries are granted either visa exemption or visas on arrival at the airport, valid for 15-90 days, depending on the country. Officially, you need an air ticket out of Thailand, but this is rarely checked. Longer tourist visas, obtained from the Thai consulate in your home country prior to arrival, allow a 60-day stay.

Visas can be extended for 30 days at a time for B1,000 at the Immigration Bureau (120 Moo 3, Thanon Chaengwattana; tel: 0 2141 9889; www.immigration.go.th; Mon–Fri 8.30am–4.30pm), or you can leave the country (even for half an hour) and

return in order to receive another visa on entry. In total, tourists are allowed to stay in Thailand for a cumulative period not exceeding 90 days within any six-month period from the date of first entry.

People seeking a work permit can apply for a non-immigrant visa, which is good for 90 days. A letter of guarantee is needed from the Thai company you intend to work for, and this visa can be obtained from a Thai consulate at home.

Overstaying your visa carries a daily fine of B500 up to a maximum of B20,000, which is payable at the airport on leaving. However, staying in Thailand on an expired visa is against the law, and if the police catch you before you leave you may be jailed and deported.

W

WEBSITES

Bangkok Post: www.bangkokpost.com. The country's biggest-selling English-language daily newspaper.

Bangkok Tourist: www.bk.asia-city.com. Good range of sites and cultural information from the Bangkok Metropolitan Authority.

BK Magazine: www.aziacity.com/bk. Site of a weekly listings magazine with features, events and restaurant reviews.

Khao San Road: www.khaosanroad. com. Backpackers' resource with accommodation, work advice, etc.

TAT: www.tourismthailand.org. Official tourist authority website *(see p.105)*.

(see p.105)

Above from far left: line of longtail boats; warm Thai greeting; navigating the Chao Phraya.

Women Travellers Thais tend to be non-confrontational, and Thailand is generally safe for women travellers in terms of both casual harassment and serious assault. That said, it is best to avoid walking alone at night on island beaches.

Thailand is no longer the ultra cheap destination of backpacker folklore but Bangkok still has very affordable accommodation, particularly around the Khao San Road area, where you may even find a pool included for 500 baht a night. Further up the chain, development has been rapid, which means prices remain competitive from mid-range to luxury and there's an increasing spread of boutique properties around the city.

Rattanakosin

Arun Residence

38 Soi Pratoo Nok Yoong; tel: 0 2221 9158; www.arunresidence.com; $$

Situated in an old Sino-Portuguese mansion on a residential street, this tiny boutique hotel is just a short walk from Wat Pho. One side of it perches on the bank of the Chao Phraya River, offering views of Wat Arun. Its Euro-Thai restaurant, Deck, is an atmospheric spot.

Chakrabongse Villas

396 Thanon Maharat; tel: 0 2225 0139; www.thaivillas.com; $$$$

This compound was built in 1908 as the home of a Thai prince (some of his family still live here). Four Thai-style villas in an elegant setting overlooking the river and Wat Arun. Beautiful gardens and a secluded pool add to its appeal, as does close proximity to the Grand Palace, a 15-minute walk away.

Thonburi

Anantara Bangkok Riverside Resort & Spa

257 Thanon Charoen Nakhon; tel: 0 2476 0022; www.bangkok-riverside.anantara.com; $$$

It is a peaceful 15-minute boat ride to this resort with lush grounds and a river-front pool, making it a relaxing escape from the city. There are regular shuttle boats downtown, but if you would rather not go anywhere, there are six restaurants, three bars and the divine Mandara Spa. The River-side Terrace hosts Thai dance-drama over dinner.

The Peninsula Bangkok

333 Thanon Charoen Nakhon; tel: 0 2861 2888; www.peninsula.com; $$$$

Being on the 'wrong' side of the river, the views have the advantage of the downtown lights. The decor is international and contemporary with neat Asian undertones, and all rooms overlook the Chao Phraya. The superb Mei Jiang is one of the best Chinese restaurants in the city. Free shuttle boat to the Saphan Taksin Skytrain Station.

Chinatown

Grand China Princess

215 Thanon Yaowarat; tel: 0 2224 9977; www.grandchina.com; $$

Smart rooms with good river and city views are a major draw at this large

Price for a double room without breakfast and taxes:	
$$$$	over B8,000
$$$	B4,000–8,000
$$	B2,000–4,000
$	below B2,000

hotel, as is the revolving restaurant on the 25th floor. Set amid Chinatown bustle, it's 10 minutes to Old City sights by taxi, or on foot to the ferry pier.

Shanghai Mansion

479–81 Thanon Yaowarat; tel: 0 2221 2121; www.shanghaimansion.com; $$

A classy boutique hotel in a part of town often written off as lacking decent lodgings. Rooms have lovely over-the-top chinoiserie, four-poster beds and vibrant hues, many reflecting those in nearby market alleyways. It is feng shui heaven with free internet access and a spa.

Pathumwan
A-One Inn

13–15 Soi Kasemsan 1, Thanon Rama I; tel: 0 2215 3029; www.aoneinn.com; $

Very basic rooms, but with satellite TV and air conditioning and a good price for an area so close to Siam Square shops and the Skytrain. Internet café with Wi-fi, and a laundry service. It's a popular spot, but if it's full this street has other similar options.

Conrad Bangkok

All Seasons Place, 87 Thanon Withayu; tel: 0 2690 9999; www.conradhotels.com; $$$

Oozing class and amenities, this top-notch hotel is adjacent to the All Seasons Place shopping centre. Spacious rooms are furnished with Thai silk and woods, with high-speed internet access and large bathrooms. An excellent choice of outlets includes

the Diplomat jazz bar. For longer stays, the serviced apartments are a better deal.

Grand Hyatt Erawan

494 Thanon Ratchadamri; tel: 0 2254 1234; www.bangkok.grand.hyatt.com; $$$

Close to Chidlom Skytrain Station, this is perfect for downtown shopping, and is located beside the Erawan Shrine. A favourite with Bangkok socialites, it has imposing style, from monolithic columns in the lobby to a garden spa on the roof. The basement restaurant-nightclub Spasso is one of Bangkok's few successful hotel nightspots.

VIE Hotel

117/39–40 Thanon Phaya Thai; tel: 0 2309 3939; www.accorhotels.com; $$

This new hotel has modern, elegant rooms fitted with LCD TVs, computers, Wi-fi and lots of nice Asian design touches. A few minutes' walk from downtown malls like MBK and Siam Paragon. There's a rooftop pool bar to relax at and a decent international restaurant, also with good views.

Sukhumvit
Atlanta

78 Sukhumvit Soi 2; tel: 0 2252 1650; www.theatlantahotelbangkok.com; $

A quirky 1950s throwback, this was Sukhumvit's first hotel. Rich in character, with an exquisite period interior, it also has a strong moral ethos that holds no truck with sex tourists and allows no visitors. Pitched at 'suitable'

Peak Periods
Advance hotel bookings are advised for the holiday periods at Christmas, New Year and Chinese New Year (Feb or Mar), and for the Songkran festival in mid-April.

Choosing a Hotel
Many moderately priced hotels in Bangkok have excellent facilities, and even budget hotels often have a swimming pool and at least one decent food outlet. Those on a tight budget will find numerous guesthouses with clean accommodation plus air conditioning and en suite bathrooms.

guests, it describes itself as 'untouched by post-modern primitivism'. There is a pool in landscaped gardens and a good Thai restaurant.

Emporium Suites

622 Sukhumvit Soi 24; tel: 0 2664 9999; www.emporiumsuites.com; $$$

Located above the Emporium mall, and connected to the Phrom Phong Skytrain Station, this dapper serviced apartment complex offers options from studio and 1-bedroom suites to 3-bedroom apartments with a full range of facilities. Some rooms have views of Benjasiri Park.

The Eugenia

267 Sukhumvit Soi 31; tel: 0 2259 9011; www.theeugenia.com; $$$

This 12-suite hotel blends 19th-century old-world colonial charm with warm Thai hospitality. Many of its rooms offer four-poster beds, and all come with antique furniture and furnishings. For a ride in style, opt for a city tour or airport transfer in one of the hotel's vintage Jaguars or Mercs.

JW Marriott

4 Sukhumvit Soi 2; tel: 0 2656 7700; www.marriotthotels.com; $$$

This classy five-star hotel is just around

the corner from the risqué Nana Entertainment Plaza, but don't let that deter you. It has all the usual superior amenities, including a large fitness centre, efficient business facilities and spacious, well-appointed rooms. As befits one of the city's top hotels, it has some of the best dining – at the New York Steakhouse *(see p.118)*.

Seven

3/15 Sukhumvit Soi 31; tel: 0 2662 0951; www.sleepatseven.com; $$

Ultra-cool hotel with bar, gallery and café. It features six rooms, each with its own colour and cosmological meaning based on the Thai tradition of assigning colours to days of the week. The 7th Heaven Bar, sundeck and free Wi-fi are other advantages of this small but stylishly functional hotel.

Sheraton Grande Sukhumvit

250 Thanon Sukhumvit; tel: 0 2649 8888; www.starwood.com; $$$

A five-star property with first-rate facilities and spacious rooms with all the amenities you would expect. Well located, with a skywalk to Skytrain and metro stations, it also has a beautifully landscaped pool and an excellent spa, plus particularly good Thai and Italian restaurants, a sophisticated lounge-bar-cum-nightclub and some hot visiting jazz players at the Living Room.

Suk11 Hostel

1/33 Sukhumvit Soi 11; tel: 0 2253 5927; www.suk11.com; $

Rooms are rather bare, with no TV or fridge, but this pleasant family-run

Price for a double room without breakfast and taxes:	
$$$$	over B8,000
$$$	B4,000–8,000
$$	B2,000–4,000
$	below B2,000

Thai-style guesthouse is still a gem, and is often booked out. It sits in a row of airy Thai houses, a short walk from the Skytrain, and features lots of wood and rustic decor. Internet access available and Wi-fi in the lobby.

Silom

Dusit Thani

946 Thanon Rama IV; tel: 0 2200 9999; www.dusit.com; $$–$$$
Ideally located across from Lumphini Park, near Patpong's nightlife, and beside MRT and Skytrain stations, this was Bangkok's first luxury hotel when it opened in the 1970s. Recent refurbishments have added new millennium chic to the Asian-tinged interior. Enjoy a massage at the Devarana Spa, then float on to one of its 13 bars and restaurants, including top-floor D'Sens for impeccable French dining *(see p.119).*

Lebua at State Tower

State Tower; 1055/111 Thanon Silom; tel: 0 2624 9999; www.lebua.com; $$$
These de luxe contemporary Asian-style rooms and suites are housed in the 64-storey State Tower and have river or city view balconies. The opulent rooftop eating and drinking outlets are collectively called The Dome *(see p.61)* and include Sirocco *(see p.120)*, Mezzaluna and Breeze, as well as the sophisticated Distil Bar, all with superb city and river views.

Luxx

6/11 Thanon Decho; tel: 0 2635 8800; www.staywithluxx.com; $–$$
The choice of accommodation here runs from impressive suites and studios (with large bathrooms, hi-tech entertainment systems and picture windows overlooking a tranquil courtyard), to stylish and functional standards and doubles, with comfy beds and the usual mod cons. Each of the 13 rooms comes with a quaint wooden barrel bathtub.

Mandarin Oriental Bangkok

48 Charoen Krung Soi 40; tel: 0 2659 9000; www.mandarin oriental.com; $$$$
Bangkok's riverside Grand Dame has been hosting guests since 1876; its original Authors' Wing still has period suites and a delightful tearoom. Newer wings attract a luminous guest list that includes royalty and stars in every field from parliament to pop. The excellent Le Normandie French restaurant requires a jacket for dinner, while the Oriental Spa offers East-meets-West themes. *See also pp.35 and 120.*

Le Meridien

40/5 Thanon Surawong; tel: 0 2232 8888; www.lemeridien.com/bangkok surawong; $$–$$$
This new sleek, modernist hotel just 50m/yds from Patpong is a fully wired techno vision of brushed concrete, glass and funky nightclub lighting effects. Rooms have full wall windows, flat-screen TVs and 'rainforest' showers, while the signature restaurant Bamboo Chic fuses Thai, Japanese and Chinese cuisines to a techno soundtrack, with *sake* and *shouchu* lists alongside the wine.

Above from far left: spectacular lobby at the Grand Hyatt Erawan *(see p.111);* Somerset Maugham suite at the Mandarin Oriental.

Booking Tip
Many mid-price and top-end hotels charge a standard 7 percent VAT and 10 percent service charge, so check to see if the quoted rate includes them. Internet prices are often lower; visit hotel websites or online hotel sites like www.thailandhotels.net.

Boutique Boom

Since the late 1990s Khao San Road has steadily gone more up-market, reflecting both the fact that modern backpackers have more money than their hippie predecessors and the increasing professionalisation of the guesthouse industry. Chart, Sawasdee and Buddy Lodge, which led the trend in Khao San 'boutique' accommodation, have all bought into neighbouring properties to launch several brands on the street.

La Residence

173/8–9 Thanon Surawong; tel: 0 2266 5400; www.laresidence bangkok.com; $$

A small hotel with a friendly vibe and funky, individually decorated rooms of different sizes. It is a short cab ride to Thanon Silom, with the attractions of Patpong night market, restaurants and pubs, and also to the river, from where there are boats to many city highlights. Rooms include two modest suites, one with garden balcony views. All accommodation has Wi-fi access.

The Sukhothai

13/3 Thanon Sathorn Thai; tel: 0 2344 8888; www.sukhothai.com; $$$$

Drawing architectural inspiration from the ancient Siamese kingdom of Sukhothai, this place was years ahead of the pack in its use of Asian detailing in a contemporary setting. Well-appointed rooms in tropical gardens with a beautiful infinity pool. Facilities include the stylish Italian restaurant La Scala; one of Bangkok's best up-market Thai restaurants, Celadon; and the tastefully attired Zuk Bar.

Take a Nap

920–6 Thanon Rama 4; tel: 0 2637 0015; www.takeanaphotel.com; $

Price for a double room without breakfast and taxes:	
$$$$	over B8,000
$$$	B4,000–8,000
$$	B2,000–4,000
$	below B2,000

Take a Nap has basic but attractive rooms, each with an artistic theme, such as Japanese waves, Pop Art, and the child-like Happy Forest, painted on the wall. There is air conditioning and a few TV stations available, but no fridges or wardrobes. It is close to the Patpong night market and just a five-minute walk to Skytrain and subway stations.

Banglamphu

Buddy Lodge

265 Thanon Khao San; tel: 0 2629 4477; www.buddylodge.com; $–$$

Khao San's pioneering boutique hotel at the beginning of the century, Buddy Lodge has a rooftop swimming pool, fitness room and a well-run spa. The rooms are more cute than plush, but are en suite with wood walls, louvred windows, small balconies and satellite TV. Located in a mini mall with bars, shops and a McDonald's downstairs.

Old Bangkok Inn

609 Thanon Phra Sumen; tel: 0 2629 1785; www.oldbangkok inn.com; $$

With teak furniture and fittings this 10-room hotel is a gem of traditional Thai character, set in a late 19th-century royal home. The rooms and suites each have a floral theme, and some have split level accommodation with sleeping areas in the loft. Installed in each room are satellite TVs, DVD players, broadband internet, and even computers. It is close to the Golden Mount and well situated for the Old City attractions.

Viengtai Hotel

42 Thanon Rambuttri; tel: 2 280 5434–45; www.viengtai.co.th; $$

This large, recently renovated hotel has smartly decorated rooms all with en suite bathrooms and cable TV, and there are a few family suites. There is a small outdoor swimming pool, wireless internet access in the lobby and a buffet restaurant.

West of Bangkok

Baan Sukchoke Country Resort

103 Moo 5 Damnoen Saduak; tel: 032 254 301; $

There is a pleasing feel to these simple but clean wooden bungalows arranged around a canal. The surroundings are like an informal open-air museum with traditional boats and farming equipment scattered around. The alfresco café serves decent Thai food. You can also arrange to visit the local floating market by boat from here.

Kanchanaburi

Felix River Kwai

9/1 Moo 3 Thamakham; tel: 0 3455 1000; www.felixriverkwai.co.th; $$

A comfortable resort-style hotel in a pretty riverside garden setting, the Felix has been around for a long time and is showing some signs of wear, but it is still the first choice of accommodation in town. The de luxe rooms facing the river are very romantic, and the large pool is perfect for lounging. You can walk from the hotel to the Bridge on the River Kwai.

Hua Hin

Baan Talay Dao

2/10 Soi Takiab; tel: 0 3253 6024; www.baantalaydao.com; $$–$$$

The 'House Between the Sea and Stars' is a resort built around a 90-year-old teak house on the road towards Khao Takiab. The accommodation is mainly studio rooms, but there are also several nice villas and suites arranged around a pool and jacuzzi area. Garden pathways lead past small water features to the beach. The restaurant serves both Thai and international food.

Sofitel Centara Hua Hin

1 Damnernkasem Road; tel: 0 3251 2021; www.sofitel.com; $$$–$$$$

This gorgeous hotel retains the white colonial elegance from the 1920s when it was built to house distinguished guests at the newly created royal retreat of Hua Hin. Lush gardens are the backdrop for a choice of villas or handsome rooms, while infinity pools offer prime sunbathing spots by the beach.

Pattaya

Rabbit Resort

Dongtan Beach, Jomtien; tel: 0 3825 1730; www.rabbitresort.com; $$–$$$

This beach resort had local village sensibilities in mind when it designed cosy Thai-style houses and bungalows amid pretty palm-tree gardens. Villa accommodation is also available, with two en suite bedrooms. All options are individually decorated with original artworks and antiques. Two pools, a restaurant and an ocean-side grill.

Above from far left: Sheraton Grande Sukhumvit's spa *(see p.112)*; Asian detailing at the Sukhothai.

Bangkok's dining options are wonderfully varied. There is tasty Thai street food served at plastic tables for as little as 20 baht a dish; tiny cafés galore; riverside garden diners; and luxury roof top restaurants where you can blow thousands. The city now has two branches of Thai restaurants with Michelin star connections, while international options include French, Italian, Chinese, Japanese, Indian, Mexican and a whole host of others.

Chinatown

Soi Texas

Soi Padung Dao; 9am–2am; $–$$

Famed for its food, this small Chinatown lane is named after the Texas Suki restaurant 50m/yds on the right. It also has two packed stalls at the mouth of the *soi*, Rut and Lek and T & K (open from 6pm). They serve great curried crab and seafood that is superb charcoal-grilled or fried with garlic and chilli.

Pathumwan

Gaggan

68/1 Soi Langsuan; tel: 0-2652-1700; daily 6–11pm; $$$

In a summer-house interior of white woods and rattan this 'progressive Indian' has El Bulli-inspired molecular cooking techniques in dishes like

A meal for one person, excluding drinks and taxes:

$$$$	over B1,500
$$$	B700–1,500
$$	B200–700
$	below B200

roasted foie gras with raspberry chutney. It's interesting, but the excellent traditional fare such as *bhunna* mutton curry is far more successful. The small roof terrace upstairs is a good spot for pre- or post-dinner drinks.

Grossi

InterContinental Bangkok, 973 Thanon Ploenchit; tel: 0 2656 0444; grossitrattoriabangkok.grossi. com.au; daily 9am–midnight; $$$

Trattoria franchise of star Aussie chef Guy Grossi with an elegant deli ambience. There's a floor of large black and white checks, marble counter displays of wines, bread and cold meats, and a menu that eschews obvious Italian exports for dishes like *burrata* salad with anchovies and pressed beef with chocolate and orange zest.

La Monita Taqueria

888/26 Mahatun Plaza, Thanon Ploenchit; tel: 0 2650 9581; daily 11.30am–10pm; $–$$

Five-table Mexican diner with cheap decor, good food and a friendly atmosphere. All the usual burritos, nachos, wings and Mexi or Cali tacos to wash down with mojitos and beer, plus good smoky guacamole and free corkage.

Red Sky

Centara Grand Hotel, 999/99 Thanon Rama I; tel: 0 2100 6101; daily 11.30am–2.30pm, 6.30–11.30pm; $$$$

Alfresco rooftop restaurant with great views. Serves huge steaks of dry-aged New York strip loin, roast Boston

lobster, Bresse pigeon stuffed with dried fruit and other tasty but expensive fare.

Sra Bua

Siam Kempinski Hotel, Thanon 991/9 Rama I; tel: 0 2162 9000; Mon–Fri noon–2.30pm, daily 6–11pm; $$$$

This outlet of Copenhagen's Michelin-starred Kiin Kiin has a rather masculine, businesslike interior, but displays a thrilling modern slant on Thai food with dishes like green curry mousse, *tom klong* soup served as jellies, and red curry ice cream.

Sukhumvit

Le Beaulieu

50 Sukhumvit Soi 19; tel: 0 2204 2004; www.le-beaulieu.com; daily 11.30am–2.30pm and 6.30–10.30pm; $$$

With dishes like slow-cooked mushroom ragout and New Zealand roast tenderloin in a sauce of veal jus, shallots, white port and pancetta, chef Hervé Frerard has forged one of the best reputations in town for French cuisine. The cosy stone tiling and Mediterranean blue decor sets a relaxing tone to enjoy wine with a good range of imported cheeses.

Bed Supperclub

26 Sukhumvit Soi 11; tel: 0 2651 3537; www.bedsupperclub.com; daily 7.30pm–1am; $$$$

This extraordinary tubular construction has an all-white interior of beds and cushions that diners lounge on while they eat inspired fusion cuisine. Mixed-media shows accompany meals on multi-choice three-course set menus including dishes like Moroccan cous cous with chilli jam and tuna steak coated in the North African marinade *chermoula*. Next door is Bed Bar, one of the city's top clubs (see p.20).

Bo.lan

42 Soi Pichai Ronnarong, Sukhumvit Soi 26; tel: 0 2260 2962; www.bo.lan.com; Tue–Sun 6.30–10.30pm; $$$

Bo and Dylan set up this cute townhouse operation fresh from working at London's Michelin-starred Thai restaurant Naam, and have a similar focus on traditional recipes. The short menu starts with a herb liquor, *ya dong*, and continues through mysterious regional flavours in dishes like sweet cured pork in coconut cream and deep-fried fish with an eye-watering spicy-sour dipping sauce.

Crêpes & Co

18 Sukhumvit Soi 12; tel: 0 2251 2895; www.crepes.co.th; daily 9am–midnight; $$

A relaxed and reliable crêperie that specialises in unusual international fillings along with the crêpe suzettes. It also serves tajines, *briouattes* and other Moroccan dishes, plus Greek favourites like *melizana salata*. The tasteful wooden interior, with a Berber-style tented ceiling and world music on the sound system, creates a cosmopolitan atmosphere. There is a popular brunch on offer, too, and garden seating.

Above from far left: all-white interior of Bed Supperclub; Hazara entrance (see p.118).

Table Etiquette
Eat Thai food with a fork and spoon, using the fork to push food onto the spoon. Chopsticks are used only for Chinese and noodle dishes. Most Thai meals have dishes placed in the middle of the table to be shared by all; the larger the group, the more dishes you can try. Put a helping of rice onto your plate, together with small portions of various dishes at the side. It is polite to take just a little at a time.

Service Tax
The more expensive
restaurants add a
service charge of
10 percent. Tipping
is not customary,
although it is usual
to leave the small
change left over
from the bill.

Hazara

29 Sukhumvit Soi 38; tel: 0 2713
6048/9; www.facebars.com; daily
11.30am–2.30pm, 6–10.30pm; $$$

Tasty North Indian fare, such as pep-
pery *khadai kheenga* (shrimps stir-fried
with bell peppers), is served in a glor-
ious setting embellished with Asian
antiques and artefacts. Hazara is set in
a series of houses in a traditional Thai-
style complex that also includes the
trendy Face Bar, a Thai restaurant called
Lan Na Thai, a pâtisserie and a spa.

Long Table

Floor 25, The Column Residence,
Sukhumvit Soi 16; tel: 0 2302
2557/9; www.longtablebangkok.
com; daily 11am–2am; $$$

Fantastic city views and a long table for
communal-style dining are the focal
points for this classy modern Thai
restaurant. It has panache, both in
interior decor and dishes such as crab
in yellow curry and foie gras with
tamarind, which are both hits from a
menu served Western-style in individual portions.

Nasir Al-Masri

4/6 Sukhumvit Soi 3/1; tel: 0 2253
5582; www.restaurant-shishah-nasir.
com; daily 24 hours; $

A meal for one person,
excluding drinks and taxes:

$$$$	over B1,500
$$$	B700–1,500
$$	B200–700
$	below B200

This area is often called Soi Arab
because of its Middle Eastern operations selling kebabs and Lebanese-style
dips. Along with the standard skewers,
'Nasir the Egyptian' also has specialities from home, such as *fuul* (mashed
beans in oil) and *molokhaya* (a spinach-
like vegetable mixed with garlic).
Outside, men smoke shiny metal shisha
pipes. Just like downtown Cairo.

New York Steakhouse

JW Marriott, 4 Sukhumvit Soi 2; tel:
0 2656 7700; www.marriott.com;
daily 6–11pm; $$$$

A top-notch restaurant with a relaxed
atmosphere despite the formal trap-
pings of club-like dark woods and
high-backed leather chairs. Good
Manhattan clam chowder sets up the
grain-fed Angus beef, sliced at the
table from a silver trolley (the beef is
imported chilled, not frozen). There's
a long Martini list and fine wines, and
atmospheric black-and-white photos
of the Big Apple adorn the walls.
Booking is essential.

Pizzeria Limoncello

17 Sukhumvit Soi 11; tel: 0 2651
0707; daily noon–2pm and 6–11pm;
$$

There are some Italian standards on the
menu, but most people come for the big
tasty pizzas prepared in the wood-fired
oven. The summery lemon-and-blue
interior with ceiling frescoes of cherubs
amid wispy clouds is a cheery setting for
fun dining. The restaurant has the sig-
nature buzz of owner Zanotti. It's often
full, so book ahead.

Silom

Aoi

132/10–11 Silom Soi 6; tel: 0 2235 2321–2; daily 11.30am–2pm and 6–10pm; $$–$$$

Black stone walkways give a cool calm to this unfussy restaurant serving excellent Japanese food. Downstairs is a sushi bar, with two floors of private and semi-private rooms above (available at a surcharge). As with all Japanese restaurants, set meals are much cheaper than ordering à la carte. There is another branch in Emporium shopping mall.

China House

Mandarin Oriental, 48 Charoen Krung Soi 40; tel: 0 2659 9000; www. mandarinoriental.com; daily 11.30am–2pm and 7–10pm; $$$

The beautiful 1930s Shanghainese Art Deco interior features red lanterns, carved wood and ebony pillars. Miniature black-and-white photos and Chinese calligraphy cover the walls; a brass samovar steams in the central tearoom. It's a wonderful setting for top-quality dishes like hot-and-sour soup with fresh herbs and sweet lobster meat, or hand-pulled noodles with green crab claw.

Concerto

661 Fl 1–2 Thanon Silom; tel: 0 2266 5333; www.niusonsilom.com; daily 5pm–1am; $$$

The restaurant at Niu's on Silom jazz bar *(see p.21)* is an intimate, upscale Italian place of candle-lit tables. Da Vinci on the walls, and a piano trio playing in the corner. The modern approach to cooking belies the classical tone with dishes like tian of Scottish salmon, pikeperch and *burrata* with tomato confiture. It also has terrace seating in a European-style piazza.

D'Sens

Dusit Thani Hotel, 946 Thanon Rama IV; tel: 0 2236 9999; www.dusit.com; Mon–Fri 11.30am–2.30pm, Mon–Sat 6–10.30pm; $$$$

A branch of the three-Michelin-starred Le Jardin des Sens in Montpellier, France, D'Sens is full of delicate and delicious surprises. The chefs work wonders in the kitchen, producing dishes such as Brittany Blue Lobster terrine with mango and smoked duck breast. The porcini mushrooms and duck-liver ravioli in a frothy truffle *sabayon* is superb, as are the desserts. And to top it off there are good views from the windows.

Eat Me

1/F, 1/6 Piphat Soi 2, off Thanon Convent; tel: 0 2238 0931; daily 3pm–1am; $$$

An extremely popular Australian-run restaurant, often exhibiting the work of edgy young artists from the nearby H Gallery. The modern eclectic menu features dishes such as charred scallops with mango, herb salad, pickled onions and citrus dressing. Low lighting and a fragmented layout lend a sense of intimacy. On pleasantly cool nights ask for a table on the terrace. There is a decent wine list.

Dinner Cruises
To combine a Thai dinner with sight-seeing on a cruise along the Chao Phraya River, contact Yok Yor (www.yokyor.co.th) or Manohra Cruises (tel: 0 2476 0022; www.manohra cruises.com).

Harmonique

22 Charoen Krung Soi 34; tel: 0 2237 8175; Mon–Sat 10am–10pm; $–$$

This cute restaurant occupies several old Chinese shophouses and spills into leafy courtyards. As there is a large contingent of Western diners the spices are too quiet for many Thais, but the curries and spicy salads are generally tasty. It is a relaxing place to hang out if you feel like an 'out of town' ambience, and is very handy for the riverside hotels.

Nahm

Metropolitan Hotel, 27 Thanon Sathorn Tai; tel: 0 2625 3333; daily noon–2pm, 6.30pm–10.30pm; $$$$

This 2010 newcomer is a branch of Europe's first Michelin-starred Thai restaurant, run by Australian chef David Thompson. The ultra traditional menu tours the regions and includes intriguing flavour blends like northern pork, prawn and tamarind relish served with braised mackerel, sweet pork, crispy acacia and soft boiled eggs. Sit inside or by the outdoor pool.

Le Normandie

Mandarin Oriental, 48 Charoen Krung Soi 40; tel: 0 2236 0400; www.mandarinoriental.com; Mon–Sat noon–2.30pm, daily 7–10.30pm; $$$$

It's all about formal French dining with concoctions such as smoked eel, with eel mousse and caviar on beetroot carpaccio; and goose liver dome with Périgord truffles that verge on brilliance. In the stately marmalade-coloured interior, crystal chandeliers hang from a quilted silk ceiling, while full-length windows overlook the Chao Phraya River. Top-notch wine list and quiet piano music. Jackets required.

Sirocco

63/F, Lebua at State Tower, 1055/111 Thanon Silom; tel: 0 2624 9555; www.thedomebkk.com; daily 6pm–1am; $$$$

This spectacular 200m (656ft) high rooftop restaurant has a breathtaking panorama of the river. The striking Greco-Roman architecture and resident jazz band add to the sense of occasion. The Mediterranean food can be inconsistent, but is often excellent. Also part of The Dome complex, classy Distil Bar has good seafood; stylish Mezzaluna offers Italian cuisine; and Breeze serves an enticing modern Asian menu. Great for a memorable splash out. *See also pp.61–2.*

Somboon Seafood

169/7–11 Thanon Surawong; tel: 0 2233 3104; daily 4–11pm; $$$

Come to this no-frills café outlet on four floors, with tubular metal furniture, for very good Chinese-style seafood. Fat curried crabs and prawns devoured with spicy *nam jim* dipping sauce are favourites, along with whole

A meal for one person, excluding drinks and taxes:	
$$$$	over B1,500
$$$	B700–1,500
$$	B200–700
$	below B200

fish cooked every which way. The canteen-like service won't win awards, but the food just might.

Zanotti

G/F, Saladaeng Colonnade, 21/2 Soi Sala Daeng; tel: 0 2636 0002; www.zanotti-ristorante.com; daily 11.30am–2pm and 6–10.30pm; $$$

Chef-owner Gianmaria Zanotti has created a restaurant that people visit for the buzz as much as the food. The Italian fare includes more than 20 pasta dishes and quality seafood and steaks charcoal-grilled over orange wood from Chiang Mai in the north of Thailand. A good selection of wines is offered by the glass. The chic wine bar Vino di Zanotti opposite also serves a full menu and has live jazz.

Banglamphu

Chabad House

108/1 Soi Ram Buttri; tel: 0 2282 6388; Sun–Thur noon–9pm, Fri noon–4.30pm; $

Run as a charitable business by the synagogue in the same building, this Israeli café offers nicer surroundings than most other Middle Eastern-style eateries in the neighbourhood. And all the food is kosher of course. They have good falafel, salads, humous and the usual tahini-based dips to accompany a wide choice of main dishes. Just a short walk from Khao San Road.

May Kaidee

117/1 Thanon Tanao; tel: 0 2281 7137; www.maykaidee.com; daily 9am–11pm; $

May has a sound reputation for her vegetarian Thai standards. Northeastern dishes (with mushrooms, tofu and soya beans) and *massaman* curry (with tofu, potatoes and peanuts) are popular selections. Loved your meal? Learn how to cook it yourself by booking one of May's cooking lessons. To find this place, take the street next to Burger King and turn left. There is a second outlet 50m/yds away and another at 33 Thanon Samsen.

Pen Thai Food

229 Soi Rambuttri (pier Phra Athit; map C3); tel: 0 2282 2320; daily 7am–7.30pm; $

Khun Sitichai has had this spot since 1980, long before the first backpackers arrived. His menu has changed little. The spicy catfish curry, soups and deep-fried fish are still displayed outside in metal pots and trays in street-stall fashion and there are a few tables to sit at. And at B20–40 per dish, the prices haven't changed much either.

Thip Samai

313 Thanon Maha Chai; tel: 0 2221 6280; daily 5.30pm–3.30am; $

Located close to the Golden Mount, this is a very basic but legendary café that does several versions (and nothing else) of *pad Thai*, fried noodles with dried shrimps, roasted peanuts and bean sprouts, that is often claimed as Thailand's national dish. Options run from the traditional to 'Superb', made with fresh prawns and wrapped in a fried-egg casing.

Bangkok's nightlife scene is large and varied, running from itinerant beer bars in the back of camper vans to hi-tech dance clubs and sophisticated cocktail venues with breathtaking city views. Live music includes ska, jazz, blues and screeds of pop, plus a good opera company, while theatre takes in contemporary dance, traditional puppetry and the world famous ladyboy cabaret. Good places to hang out are Thanons Khao San, Ratchadaphisek, Sukhumvit, Silom and the busy lanes of Soi Thonglor. Silom Sois 2 and 4 have lively gay oriented options. Below is a very small selection of the most celebrated venues.

Music

Ad Here
13 Thanon Samsen; tel: 08-9769-4613; free.

Musicians (including surprises like Charlie Musselwhite) turn up to jam blues and jazz in a tiny bar. Close to Khao San Road, there's a laid-back vibe and a mix of Thai and Western clients.

Niu's on Silom
661 Fl 1-2 Thanon Silom; tel: 0-2266-5333; www.niusonsilom.com; free.

An intimate lounge bar with leather armchairs, candle-lit tables and great acoustics. Most styles from Latin to post-bop, with occasional top international acts. Dine in the club, on the terrace or in upstairs Italian restaurant.

Saxophone Pub
3/8 Thanon Phaya Thai; tel: 0-2246-5472; www.saxophonepub.com; free.

A lively two-floor venue. The mixed but mainly Thai crowd enjoys a pubby atmosphere with balcony views. They get to see some of the best local jazz, R&B, soul and funk in town.

Nightlife

Bed Bar
26 Sukhumvit Soi 11; tel: 0-2651-3537; www.bedsupperclub.com; charge.

This space-age elliptical building has a restaurant and dance club. The latter has a mix of imported DJs like Kenny Dope, Gilles Peterson and Sandy Rivera and regular theme nights, including electro, hip hop, performance art and models nights.

Cheap Charlie's
1 Sukhumvit Soi 11; tel: 0-2253-4648; free.

Minimalism reaches new heights – no roof, no walls – just a bar and a few stools in the street. It's cheap, and typical of the local penchant for setting up business wherever the mood takes you.

Club Culture
Thanon Ratchadamnoen Klang; tel: 08-9497-8422; www.club-culture-bkk.com; charge.

Three floors for visiting overseas artists and homespun DJs like Sweet, Kristian and Gene Kasidit. The music ranges from electro, garage and drum 'n' bass to hip-hop, house and disco.

LED Club
RCA Block C; tel: 0-2203-1043; www.808bangkok.com; charge.

Club Information
Thai Ticketmajor (tel: 02-262-3456; www.thaiticketmajor.com) is a good resource to check for upcoming events. When going to clubs, always carry a copy of your passport to prove your age.

Formerly called 808, this popular club relaunched in 2011, with brick and steel innards and an ace sound system. International DJs include the likes of Tiesto and Grandmaster Flash.

Q Bar

34 Sukhumvit Soi 11; tel: 0-2252-3274; www.qbarbangkok.com; charge.

Modelled after a New York lounge bar, this stylishly dark and just-seedy-enough two-floor venue plays cool dance music by both local and imported talent. Many people come for the legendary drinks menu, which features 50 brands of vodka alone.

Sky Bar/Distil

State Tower, 1055 Thanon Silom; tel: 0-2624-9555; www.thedomebkk.com; free.

Sixty-four floors up, Sky Bar is on the roof, the open-air extension of Sirocco restaurant. Distil has spectacular river views from a small balcony, and a chilled ambience. High flyers enjoy champagne and oysters at translucent onyx tables.

Theatre

Calypso

Asia Hotel, 296 Thanon Phaya Thai; tel: 0-2216-8937; www.calypso cabaret.com; charge.

One of the city's best *katoey* (transsexual) cabarets performed by sequinned artistes who have gone through various stages of sex-change. Shows (8.15pm and 9.45pm), include anything from Marilyn Monroe impersonators to Thai classical dance.

Patravadi Theatre

69/1 Soi Wat Rakhang; Thanon Arun Amarin; tel: 0-2412-7287; www.patravaditheatre.com; charge.

The nucleus of the Thai contemporary theatre scene, which melds traditional and modern dance and drama. As well as special performances throughout the year, there are dinner shows in the riverside Studio 9 (Fri–Sat nights).

Sala Chalerm Krung Theatre

66 Thanon Charoen Krung; tel: 0-2222-1854; charge.

A convenient space to see Thai classical theatre as it hosts *khon* masked drama performances on Friday and Saturday from 7pm. It's unusual to see this in a theatre; most other shows are in hotels or themed tourist spots.

Tawandang German Brewery

462/61 Thanon Rama III; tel: 0-2678-1114; www.tawandang.com; free.

Not a German brewery (although they have German beers and food) but a pub-cum-theatre with an eclectic programme of Thai-Western music and cabaret. The house band plays a mix of traditional and modern, while the rest of the night is taken over by costumed dancers, magic acts and even ballet.

Thailand Cultural Centre

Thanon Ratchadaphisek; tel: 0-2247-0028; charge.

Poor acoustics but it's one of the few places to stage performances by the Bangkok Opera (www.bangkok-opera.com) and Symphony Orchestra. It also has pop, rock and jazz concerts.

Above from far left: Bed Supperclub's impressive tubular elliptical structure; Q Bar.

Festival Venue
The Thailand Cultural Centre *(see left)* is the main venue for the International Festival of Dance and Music each September.

CREDITS

Insight Step by Step Bangkok
Written by: Howard Richardson
Series Editor: Carine Tracanelli
Cartography Editors: Zoë Goodwin
and James Macdonald
Picture Manager: Steven Lawrence
Art Editor: Ian Spick
Photography: All by APA: Jeremy Hou, Jason
Lang, Marcus Wilson Smith and Peter Stuckings,
except Luca Invernizzi Tettoni 22T, 49; M.C.
Piya Rangsit 22B; Derrick Lim/APA 33TR;
Francis Dora 34TL; iStockphoto.com 10/1 & 2,
11/2, 13/1 & 2, 26/1, 28/1, 32/2, 37/1, 46/1, 52/1
& 2, 65/1, 76/1, 82/2, 85/1, 89/1, 91/1, 93/1,
96/1, 97/1, 105, 108/1, 110/1 & 2
Front cover: main image: photolibrary.com;
bottom left and right: iStockphoto.com.
Printed by: CTPS–China

DISTRIBUTION

Worldwide
**APA Publications GmbH & Co. Verlag KG
(Singapore branch)**
7030 Ang Mo Kio Ave 5
08-65 Northstar @ AMK, Singapore 569880
E-mail: apasin@singnet.com.sg

UK and Ireland
**Dorling Kindersley Ltd
(a Penguin Company)**
80 Strand, London, WC2R 0RL, UK
E-mail: sales@uk.dk.com

United States
Ingram Publisher Services
One Ingram Blvd, PO Box 3006
La Vergne, TN 37086-1986
E-mail: customer.service@ingrampublisher
services.com

Australia
Universal Publishers
PO Box 307
St. Leonards, NSW 1590
E-mail: sales@universalpublishers.com.au

CONTACTING THE EDITORS

We would appreciate it if readers would alert us
to errors or outdated information by writing to
us at insight@apaguide.co.uk or Apa Publications,
PO Box 7910, London SE1 1WE, UK.

www.insightguides.com

THE WORLD OF
INSIGHT GUIDES

Different people need different kinds of travel information.
Some want background facts. Others seek personal
recommendations. With a variety of different products – Insight
Guides, Insight City Guides, Step by Step Guides, Smart Guides,
Insight Fleximaps and our new Great Breaks series –
we offer readers the perfect choice.

Insight Guides will turn your visit into an experience.

www.insightguides.com

INDEX